GUARDIANS of the WORD

Dave & Neta,

To my fellow lovers of the Word & God's work.

God bless you for your inspiring books.

Susan Moore

GUARDIANS
of the WORD

SUSAN MOORE

3P

Page & Pixel Publications
www.pageandpixelpublications.com

Guardians of the Word
© **2021 Susan Moore**
Page & Pixel Publications
pageandpixelpublications.com

Scripture taken from the New King James Version®. Copyright© 1982 by Thomas Nelson, Inc. Used by permission. All rights reserved.

Bible/Sword cover photo by iStock. Used by permission. Portraits are from Wikimedia Commons and are in the public domain.

Publisher's Cataloging-in-Publication Data
Moore, Susan D.
  GUARDIANS OF THE WORD
/ Susan D. Moore
     pages cm

  ISBN 978-1-7377490-0-4 (softbound : alk. paper) 1. Bible translators 2. Bible versions 3. Missionary biographies 4. Apologetics 5. Christian inspiration

Printed in the United States of America

Acknowledgments

With deep gratitude to Mary Beyer, Marsha Bradley, Mark Meier, and Matt Schroeder for taking the time to read through this manuscript and provide insight, guidance, and correction.

Words are inadequate to express my appreciation to my always supportive husband and daughter. Your limitless encouragement helped me to go on when the way seemed impossible.

Contents

The words of the Lord are pure words,
Like silver tried in a furnace of earth,
Purified seven times.
You shall keep them, O Lord,
You shall preserve [guard] them
from this generation forever.
Psalm 12:6-7

1

In the Beginning . . . It is Finished

How We Got Our Bible

The law of the Lord is perfect, converting the soul; The testimony of the Lord is sure, making wise the simple; The statutes of the Lord are right, rejoicing the heart; The commandment of the Lord is pure, enlightening the eyes; The fear of the Lord is clean, enduring forever; The judgments of the Lord are true and righteous altogether. (Psalm 19:7-9)

The Holy Bible, God's Word, The Scriptures, Holy Writ, The Book of Books, The Old and New Testaments. Oh, how we love the Bible! Without dispute the Bible is a remarkable piece of literature. It has been translated into more languages than any other book. More copies of it have been printed, sold, or distributed than any other writing in the entire history of the world. Christians who revere the Bible would describe it as inspired, inerrant, and the final and complete revelation of God to mankind. We believe it to be the ultimate authority for everything pertaining to life and godliness; and that it is "profitable for doctrine, for reproof, for correction, for instruction in righteousness that the man of God may be complete, thoroughly equipped for every good work" (2 Timothy 3:16-17).

Yet today the Bible is under attack like never before. Its history and authenticity are being challenged by both secularists and the religious. Questions are raised—"Why do you think the Bible is the Word of God?" "The Bible was written a long, long time ago. How do you know what you're reading is accurate?" Many times these sincere questions can catch us off guard and even allow a whisper of doubt to creep in.

How *did* we get our Bible? A very brief summary of how the Bible came to be can reinforce the conviction that the Bible we read today can be trusted and that the Lord has protected and preserved its content down through the centuries.

The Dead Sea Scrolls

IN 1947 JUM'A ed-Dib, a Bedouin goatherd wandered the Judean desert with his brother Mohammed and their modest herd of sheep and goats. Jum'a took a quick head count and noticed one of his bleating charges had gone missing. He went off to search for it among the craggy cliffs encircling the Dead Sea in the region known as Qumran. Suddenly Jum'a saw a crevice that opened up into a cave. Peering in, he tried to determine if it was deep enough for his wayward goat to be completely concealed in the darkness. Jum'a tossed in a limestone rock in hopes of eliciting a response from the animal. Instead he heard what sounded like pottery breaking. He scrambled down into the cave to investigate where he discovered some shattered empty clay jars. There were also some intact jars with the lids still firmly affixed. Inside the containers the goatherd found nothing but some old age-darkened scrolls.

The Bedouin brothers liberated seven scrolls from their deep dark hiding place and sold them to an antiquities dealer in Bethlehem. The scrolls passed through several hands before Hebrew University Professor Eliezer Lipa Sukenik was able to get a look at them. Carefully unrolling the scrolls, the scholar was amazed to see Hebrew manuscripts one thousand years older than any existing biblical text. In his diary, Sukenik recollected:

> My hands shook as I started to unwrap one of them. I read a few sentences. It was written in beautiful biblical Hebrew. The language was like that of the Psalms, but the text was unknown to me. I looked and looked, and I suddenly had the feeling that I was privileged by destiny to gaze upon a Hebrew scroll which had not been read for more than 2,000 years. [1]

As word spread of this unprecedented discovery, treasure hunters, scholars, and archaeologists converged on the landscape surrounding the Dead Sea; and by 1955, ten other caves had been found which also contained ancient scrolls preserved in sealed pottery. Of paramount interest to Bible scholars are the 230 scrolls, manuscripts, or fragments containing every book in the Hebrew Bible (our Old Testament). These are the oldest known copies of biblical works, dating to the second century BC.[2]

Fast forward to today. Apologist and Bible scholar Dr. David Hocking likes to demonstrate how accurately the Word of God has been preserved down through the centuries. While leading tour groups in Jerusalem, he frequently takes his team to the Shrine of the Book, a museum where the Hebrew text of the Book of Isaiah, taken from the Qumran caves, is on display. Hocking relates:

> The Isaiah scroll is unraveled and it is all the way around this big glass case. We look up a given passage and I look it up in my Hebrew Bible [that I use] today and I take and I rip a page out. Forgive me, but I do. And I put the page up there on the window and let people notice the consonants and I point them out one by one. And it is amazing the effect on people! They say, "Well, those are exactly the same!" That is true, though there is over a thousand years' difference between the two. You tell me, were the Jews careful [about preserving the Word of God]? [3]

The Very First Guardians of the Word

> God, who at various times and in various ways spoke in time past to the fathers by the prophets, has in these last days spoken to us by [His] Son . . . (Hebrews 1:1-2a)

THE BOOKS OF the Old Testament are the product of at least thirty authors who wrote over a period of a thousand years or more. There is evidence within the Old Testament itself that this collection of inspired books grew gradually over time. For example: "Moses wrote all the words of the Lord" (Exodus 24:4); Samuel told the people the manner of the kingdom, and "wrote it in a book, and laid it up before the Lord" (1 Samuel 10:25); Deuteronomy says that these writings were to be kept in the side of the Ark of the Covenant (Deuteronomy 31:26). Such passages show that these God-breathed writings penned by Moses, David, and the prophets, were cherished and safely protected.

Obviously, before the invention of the printing press, all manuscripts had to be hand copied. For texts that were sacred to the Jews, this was the exclusive task of the scribes. They took their jobs very seriously. Here are a few of the regulations to which they adhered:

1. They could only use clean animal skins, both to write on, and even to bind manuscripts.
2. Each column of writing could have no less than forty-eight, and no more than sixty lines.
3. The ink must be black, and of a special recipe.
4. They must verbalize each word aloud while they were writing.
5. They must wipe the pen and wash their entire bodies before writing the word "Jehovah," every time they wrote it.
6. There must be a review within thirty days, and if as many as three pages required corrections, the entire manuscript had to be redone.
7. The letters, words, and paragraphs had to be counted, and the document became invalid if two letters touched each other. The middle paragraph, word and letter must correspond to those of the original document.
8. All old and worn documents had to be "buried" with ceremonial pomp. . . .
9. The documents could be stored only in sacred places (synagogues, etc.).
10. As no document containing God's Word could be destroyed, they were stored, or buried, in a genizah—a Hebrew term meaning "hiding place." These were usually kept in a synagogue or sometimes in a Jewish cemetery.4

What care they took to preserve the accuracy of God's Word! Thank God for their meticulous habits! Without the diligence of the often-maligned scribes, the writings of Moses and the prophets might have been lost forever.

God saw to it that the writings were protected; for in 586 BC Jerusalem was captured by the Babylonians. The Temple was looted and destroyed. Hundreds of prisoners were taken away captive. Seventy years later when the Hebrews returned to their homeland, Ezra gathered together the books of the Old Testament which had been miraculously preserved through the devastation and the exile. And they have been kept safe ever since.

> The complete volume [of the Old Testament] is associated by tradition with Ezra, and there are no valid reasons for doubting this, especially as it harmonizes with the testimony of the well-informed and representative Jew, Josephus, who, writing in the first century of the Christian Era, said that no book was added to the Jewish Scripture after the time of Malachi. [5]

This collection of authoritative writings making up the Jewish Bible consisted of twenty-two books—twenty-two letters in the Hebrew alphabet; twenty-two books compiled as the Holy Scriptures. These would be the exact same books the Lord Jesus quoted from and the apostles and the early church used for preaching and teaching, for edification, and for instruction in righteousness. And our Old Testament today contains exactly the same material, though in a slightly different order. Also a number of the Hebrew books have been divided up into separate books making the total number thirty-nine. These books are regarded as Holy Scriptures by Jews, Catholics, and Protestants. They are:

Genesis	2 Chronicles	Daniel
Exodus	Ezra	Hosea
Leviticus	Nehemiah	Joel
Numbers	Esther	Amos
Deuteronomy	Job	Obadiah
Joshua	Psalms	Jonah
Judges	Proverbs	Micah
Ruth	Ecclesiastes	Nahum
1 Samuel	Song of Solomon	Habakkuk
2 Samuel	Isaiah	Zephaniah
1 Kings	Jeremiah	Haggai
2 Kings	Lamentations	Zechariah
1 Chronicles	Ezekiel	Malachi

If there is one word which you need to put into your vocabulary when thinking about the origins of the Bible, it is the word "canon". This word refers to the books which together compose Holy Scripture. They were communicated to us by God, through special men, and became authoritative, distinct from all other writings. The Jewish canon, which is limited to the Old Testament, was publicly acknowledged long before the birth of Christ, but the official closing of the canon took place in AD 100 at a rabbinical assembly in Jamnia, thirteen miles south of modern Tel Aviv.[6] [more about canon later]

We can thank the Lord for the diligence and dedication of faithful scribes and the strict traditions of Jewish scholars for the preservation of the Word of the Lord which came to us through the Old Testament writers.

A Gift from the Greeks

ALEXANDER THE GREAT conquered a vast portion of the world around 330 BC, imposing the Greek philosophy and way of life on everyone in his extensive domain. By far the major impact upon civilization was providing the realm with a single language— *koine* or common Greek. "By the time Alexander died, in 323 BC, the world had become bilingual, and Greek was the second language everybody used. This becomes important for our story of the Bible."[7]

There is some mystery to the story of how the Greek translation of the Bible came to be. It is known that the Greeks revered knowledge above all else and so the custodians of the world famous library in Alexandria, Egypt, endeavored to compile and house every possible manuscript in the world in the Greek language. Supposedly, sometime between 285 and 100 BC, scholars were requested to come from Jerusalem to translate the books of the Jewish law from Hebrew into Greek. Six scholars from each of the twelve tribes (seventy-two) were brought to an island to work undisturbed. It is said that each scholar, working individually, finished his task in seventy-two days and miraculously all of their translations were identical! The work became known as the Septuagint—the Greek word for seventy. [8]

> The influence of the Septuagint was enormous. In the intertestamental period, persecution dispersed the Jews into "every nation under heaven," as Luke puts it in Acts. Jews spoke every known language, and many did not understand the old Hebrew of the Bible. However, everyone knew Greek. So the Septuagint met a very great need, providing the books of Moses for the Jews scattered around the world. In fact, it became the Bible. It was this book that the apostles referred to as the Word of God. [9]

The Making of the New Testament

WHEN JESUS WALKED the earth, He communicated to His followers directly—broadly and in parables to the multitudes; intimately and in detail to the apostles. He came to fulfill the law and ushered in a "new and living way" which would open up the kingdom of God to more than just one nation of chosen people.

After the Lord's resurrection the apostles continued to tell others of Christ's words and deeds. The church, the Body of Christ, grew because of their faithful oral testimony. But the apostles could not be everywhere. Paul, John, and the others began to write letters of teaching and exhortation to the churches. The congregations shared their epistles with one another. Soon it became obvious a written account of the words and life of the Savior was necessary. The four Gospels were penned by Matthew, Mark, Luke, and John. The history of the early church (Acts) followed these. And lastly John the Beloved committed the Revelation of Jesus Christ to papyrus.

> As the primitive churches had the Old Testament volume in their hands, it was a constant reminder of the need of an analogous volume of the New Testament, though everything was so very gradual and natural that it is only when the process is complete that it is realized to have been also manifestly supernatural. [10]

After the last of the apostles passed away—John in AD 100—the church entered a post-apostolic period. The leadership consisted of men who had known the apostles personally. But as time progressed, heresies and schisms crept into the church.

> Paradoxically, all these conflicts within the Christian Church served a beneficial purpose. Just as germs give rise to antibodies, which make the human body health-

ier, so heresies left the Christian church stronger. False theologies gave birth to Christian theology, and conflict forced the development of an authoritative creed, as well as the desire for a canon of scripture. [11]

As the infant church began to flex its spiritual muscles, councils met to discuss and decide upon which of the widely circulated writings would comprise the complete New Testament. In AD 315, Athanasius, the Bishop of Alexandria, was the first to identify the twenty-seven books of the New Testament which our Bibles contain today. In his Thirty-ninth Paschal Letter in AD 367, he published this list:[12]

Matthew	Ephesians	Hebrews
Mark	Philippians	James
Luke	Colossians	1 Peter
John	1 Thessalonians	2 Peter
Acts	2 Thessalonians	1 John
Romans	1 Timothy	2 John
1 Corinthians	2 Timothy	3 John
2 Corinthians	Titus	Jude
Galatians	Philemon	Revelation

Theologian and philosopher Augustine, whose writings are said to have influenced the development of Western Christianity, concurred with this list. As did Jerome, translator of the Latin Bible. (See page 23)

A council of church leaders met in Hippo Regius, North Africa (AD 393), as well as the Council in Carthage (present-day Tunisia) in AD 410, officially accepted these twenty-seven books as the complete canon of Scripture. There is nothing to be added. It is finished.

One thing must be emphatically stated. The New Testament books did not become authoritative for the Church because they were formally included in a canonical list; on the contrary, the Church included them in her canon because she already regarded them as divinely inspired, recognizing their innate worth and generally apostolic authority, direct or indirect. The first ecclesiastical councils to classify the canonical books were both held in North Africa—at Hippo Regius in 393 and at Carthage in 397—but what these councils did was not to impose something new upon the Christian communities but to codify what was already the general practice of these communities. [13]

The word *canon* or *kanon* in Greek is a measuring stick against which other items are measured (like a ruler). Dr. David Hocking lists five categories the church leaders in the fourth century used to determine if a book was to be included in the Holy Bible or not. [14]

Language— the text had to be written in one of three languages: Hebrew, Greek or Aramaic.

Authorship— Was it written by a prophet or apostle or under apostolic sanction?

Inspiration— There had to be evidence of divine inspiration either by the testimony of Jesus Himself, by the writer, by eyewitnesses to what was recorded, and/or by the witness of the Holy Spirit in the believer as he or she read the book. Was the information historically accurate?

Acceptance— Was the book widely accepted by the church-at-large? Were the believers in the local churches already acknowledging this Epistle or Gospel as the Word of God?

Completion— When the council declared the collection of twenty-seven books to be canon they were saying this (together with the thirty-nine previously accepted books of the Old Testament) is the complete Bible. Nothing could be added to it. It contained everything that needed to be known about God and His ways.

> It has been well said that the Bible is not an authorized collection of books, but a collection of authorized books. This distinction is vital. It is essential to remember that the quality which determines acceptance of a book is its possession of divine revelation. So that Canonicity did not raise a book to the position of Scripture, but recognized that it was already Scripture. [15]

> The Bible is the only infallible written revelation of God to man. It is complete, since both Old and New Testaments contain all the books God inspired for the faith and practice of future generations. . . . [N]othing more is needed; the spiritual guide to life needs no new chapters. The Author inspired a complete manual from the beginning and has preserved all of it, intact. [16]

No doubt the church leaders who attended the Council of Hippo (and other councils which met to discuss this important topic) were fallible men. But the Bible clearly teaches us this is just the kind of person that God chooses to use. In fact, God used such men to *write* the Bible. Moses misrepresented God. David was an adulterer. Peter denied the Lord. But that's what makes the Bible such an amazing book: God's words penned by human writers, meticulously copied by hand, preserved through the ages, agreed upon by councils of men who sought God's wisdom on the matter, translated into countless tongues so everyone could have access to the Word of God. This is nothing short of a miracle. And this is the Bible we have today.

> The grass withers, the flower fades, But the word of our God stands forever. (Isaiah 40:8)

A Word About the Latin Vulgate

EUSEBIUS HIRONYMUS, BETTER known simply as Jerome, is to be credited for the Bible version known as the Latin Vulgate. In his time (AD 380) there were a few unreliable Latin translations of various pieces of the New Testament in existence. Because Jerome was both a linguistic scholar and a theologian, the bishop of Rome gave him the daunting task of revising these works. The outcome was a much more accurate rendering from the Greek to Latin. After his New Testament was completed, Jerome left Rome to adopt a monastic lifestyle as he set about to translate the Old Testament into Latin. He used Origen's Hebrew text rather than the more common Septuagint (itself a translation from Hebrew to Greek) and completed the massive project in the year 405.

This work was to be the Bible in the common language. (The word *vulgate* means common.)

> . . . paradoxically it turned out to be the very instrument which blocked the road to any other vulgate. It was so highly esteemed that succeeding generations decided to forbid anyone to make any other translation, and Latin became the official language of religion, with priests, whatever their mother tongue, being taught in Latin. So the good became the enemy of the best, and ordinary people, who did not know Latin, were deprived of the Bible. [17]

HOW WE GOT THE BIBLE

500 B.C.—600 A.D.

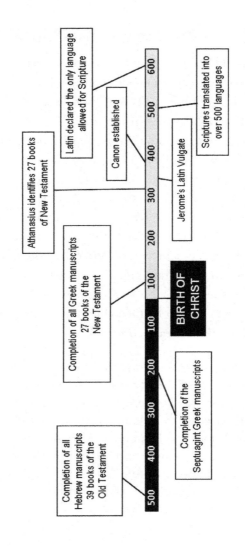

Completion of all Hebrew manuscripts 39 books of the Old Testament

Completion of the Septuagint Greek manuscripts

Completion of all Greek manuscripts 27 books of the New Testament

BIRTH OF CHRIST

Athanasius identifies 27 books of New Testament

Latin declared the only language allowed for Scripture

Canon established

Jerome's Latin Vulgate

Scriptures translated into over 500 languages

2

John Wycliffe

The Morning Star of the Reformation

What happens when the church becomes mired in sin, corruption, and false teaching? If we examine church history, we can see that God raises up brave men and women who will stand for the truth and boldly proclaim it. The preachers and prophets who dare to speak out against blatant errors in the church must count the cost of doing so. The leaders and institutions that are on the receiving end of these fiery challenges to their power and authority, often fight back. Such was the case for John Wycliffe.

For nearly two decades the pastor and professor used his pen to dispute the indulgences of the friars and the doctrines of the bishops. The church responded with threats and charges resulting in Wycliffe being branded a heretic. However, Wycliffe suffered a stroke in 1384 and died before any punishment could be exacted. But after being dead and buried for forty-one years, the anger of his enemies still burned hot against the Morning Star of the Reformation. They dug up his bones from the grave and tossed them in a fire hot enough to reduce them to ashes. The ashes were scraped together and heaved into the swift Avon River. This was the Catholic Church's futile effort to extinguish the legacy of John Wycliffe once and for all. But what was the cause of all this ire?

Wycliffe's Biography

JOHN WYCLIFFE (ALTERNATE spellings: Wyclif, Wycliff, Wiclef, Wicliffe) was born sometime between 1324 and 1330. Little is known of his early years. We know that, while a student, the plague known as the Black Death ravaged England, decimating an estimated 40% of the population in the time span of two years. This pestilence affected people from every station in life—peasants, nobility and clergy. The symptoms were gruesome and sudden. One could go to sleep feeling fine, awaken in the morning with fever, boils, and a bloody cough, and be dead within two days. Needless to say, panic gripped a large portion of the population. Many feared the wrath of God was being unleashed. Within John Wycliffe, this event produced a profound spiritual revival that reached to the core of his being. He rearranged his priorities and became more earnest in his theological pursuits. It took him nearly sixteen years to complete his education at Oxford University. In 1372 he earned a Doctor of Divinity, but by this time he was already considered the most prominent theologian and philosopher in all of England.

As a revered Oxford professor, Wycliffe frequently lectured his students on the immoralities and greed of the Catholic Church and of the friars in particular. It grieved him greatly that the free gift of salvation was being denied to the masses because of the covetousness of those holding authority. In the church's view, the clergy alone held the keys to salvation. The sinner could have the door opened for him through the mediation of the priest — for a pretty penny, of course.

> Behind the worldliness, luxury and Mammon-worship which he thought were ruining the church stood the basic evil —the church's supposed monopolistic control of the means of salvation. It was this sole possession of the keys of heaven and hell, used for financial gain, which was debauching Christendom —so Wycliffe thought— and he attacked the whole system: the necessity of auricular confession to a priest, corporal penance, pilgrimages and relic worship, financial substitutes for penance, special masses for the dead, the idea of a treasury of merit in the pope's control, and the sale of indulgences. [18]

The university's lecture halls were packed as Wycliffe skillfully defended his views against those who opposed him. His pupils and colleagues were soaking in his radical teachings. But in order to truly elicit the changes he sought, his own sphere of influence would have to expand beyond Oxford. Wycliffe came to realize that his pen could be more powerful than his pulpit. And so began the laborious task of writing and hand-copying various tracts for common distribution. This seemed "the most potent vehicle for the dissemination of revolutionary ideas."[19]

He wrote *Objections to Friars*, denouncing their "pestilent" practice of begging. In 1376 he penned *Civil Dominion*, declaring that "The pope is but a man, subject to sin: but Christ is the Lord of lords." *The Truth of the Holy Scriptures* stated that the Bible is the entire revelation of God and no further source is necessary and that all other teaching must be tested against the Bible. But the publication of his book *On the Eucharist* in 1381 addressing the doctrine of transubstantiation, which he regarded as a wholly unbiblical teaching, cost him many friendships and the support upon which he relied.

One of the last tracts he wrote took the form of an imaginary conversation between truth, falsehood, and understanding. In it he argued, "The church has fallen because she has abandoned the gospel and preferred the laws of the pope." [20]

> The Bible, Wycliffe declared, was the "highest authority for every Christian, and the standard of faith and all human perfection." All that was within it must be obeyed. All that was not—the deep patina of lore, ritual, law, hierarchy and dogma that had built up for more than a thousand years—was mere human invention and superstition. No institution that God had not sanctioned, foremost among them the papacy, was to be trusted or obeyed. . . .
>
> . . . He stressed the importance of personal faith in Christ, rather than the merits of obedience to the Church. "As belief is the first virtue and the ground of all others," he wrote, "so unbelief is the first sin of all others." This belief was not gained through intercession of the Church, he said; it flowed from the individual reading of the scripture . . ."[21]

The Catholic Church's Response

HIS OPPONENTS WERE irate and determined that one way or another, Wycliffe must be silenced. And in 1382 a council of theologians met and decreed that this and other writings contained both heresy and error.

William Courtenay, an archbishop known as the hounder of heretics, convened a council in London on May 17, 1382. "It condemned twenty-four of Wyclife's propositions as 'heretical and erroneous.' A powerful earthquake shook the city as it sat. Courtenay described the tremors as a portent of the purgings of noxious heresies from the bowels of the earth. To Wycliffe, they were proof of God's anger at the Church." [22]

So the council condemned Wycliffe, his teachings, and anyone who adhered to them. But this was a tumultuous time in both the secular and the religious world. Two popes—Urban VI and Clement VII—were vying for power, and in England the wishes of the king were often superseded by the church. In the midst of this leadership quagmire, Wycliffe managed to elude arrest and retired quietly to his parish church in Lutterworth where he spent his remaining years pursuing his deepest passion.

Wycliffe's Passion

Spurning Latin as the language of Church oppression, he wrote almost entirely in English now. Since "the truth of God standeth not in one language more than in another," he said, the Bible should be translated into English so that "it may edify the lewd people as it doth clerks in Latin ... No man is so rude a scholar but he may learn the gospel in its simplicity." He posed an apparently unanswerable question: "Why may we not write in English the gospel and other things dedicating the gospel to the edification of men's souls?" [23]

AND SO JOHN Wycliffe undertook the most important work of his life. He began to translate the Bible into the true common language of the people. Understand that the Wycliffe transla-

JOHN WYCLIFFE

tion was not a true translation from the original languages. There were two very good reasons for this. First, those original manuscripts were not available to him in fourteenth century England. And second, neither Wycliffe nor any of his fellow scholars understood Greek or Hebrew. The text he used as the basis for his work was Jerome's Latin Vulgate, the very edition the clergy used to keep the laity unenlightened to the truths of God's Word.

Incidentally, the English language was still in a state of development during this time. If you were to attempt to read a sentence of John Wycliffe's New Testament it is doubtful that it would make any sense at all. "Nyle ze deme, that se be nat demyd." Believe it or not that says, "Judge not, that ye be not judged" as the King James Version would later render it.

The conclusion of the parable of the Prodigal Son in Luke 15 can almost be deciphered if you are familiar with the passage. Wycliffe rendered verses 31 and 32 this way:

> And he seide to hym, Sone, thou art euer more with
> me, and alle my thingis ben thine. But it bihofte for to
> make feeste, and to haue ioye; for this thi brother was
> ded, and lyuede agen; he perischide, and is founden. [24]

The impact of having the Holy Scriptures in the tongue of the people cannot be overstated. Each copy took ten months to complete—painstakingly hand-copied and bound between boards—an extremely expensive endeavor. The cost for a personal copy was five thousand times the cost of purchasing a single chicken from the local market. Yet, the people were hungry for the Word of God. John Foxe reports that some laborers would trade a cartload of hay for the chance to borrow an Epistle or a Gospel for a single day.

The bishops were zealous to suppress the distribution of Wycliffe's Bible. But their determination only fueled the desire for folks to get their hands on a copy. Whether this was a result of the lure of partaking in the forbidden, or a true passion for God, or a combination of the two, we cannot be certain. However, the Catholic Church was somewhat successful in hindering its spread. Soon the production and distribution of the Scriptures were driven underground. But the Word of God cannot be bound; an unknown, but very large number of manuscripts were nevertheless produced. Each book, no doubt, passed through many hands in its lifetime. Remarkably there are still more than two hundred copies of Wycliffe's hand-copied Bible in existence today.

The Morningstar of the Reformation lived to see the Holy Bible in the English language welcomed into the hands of the common people. In the end, Wycliffe suffered a series of strokes and went to his reward in the presence of his congregation in 1384.

Wycliffe's Legacy

AFTER WYCLIFFE'S DEATH, his followers continued the work and carried the Scriptures to the people. But the hostility to Wycliffe's teachings and to his followers escalated. They came to be called "Lollards." A derivation of the Dutch word *lollen*, to mumble, it was applied to religious eccentrics and vagabonds. And the "Bible-men" (as they were more accurately named) did live as vagabonds. They roamed throughout England, not begging for alms as the friars had done, but preaching the gospel in the language of the people. They taught the priesthood of all believers, the sufficiency of the Scriptures, and the rejection of all non-biblical religious rituals. They won converts among the gentry, the merchants, artisans, peasants, and many, many women.

Respected by the common people, the Lollards were despised by the clergy. The new king Henry IV was eager to remain in favor with the church and declared himself "the protector of the church." In 1401, at the urging of the bishops, the king initiated *De Haeretico Comburendo*—an act for the burning of heretics. And the fires were lit.

William Sawtre was the first of Wycliffe's disciples to feel the flames. His crime of heresy was sealed by his bold confession, "Instead of adoring the cross on which Christ suffered, I adore Christ who suffered on it."[25] Many other martyrs followed.

Sadly, the church and the state were not satisfied with just silencing the leaders of the movement and prohibiting any Bible translation except the Latin. A further decree was issued by Parliament in 1408 making it illegal to even read the Scriptures in the privacy of their own homes.

> No one henceforth do by his own authority translate any text of Holy Scripture into the English tongue or into any other, by way of book or treatise; nor let any book or treatise now lately composed in the time of John Wycliffe, or since, or hereafter be composed, be read in whole or in part, in public or private, under pain of greater excommunication . . . He that shall do contrary to this shall likewise be punished [i.e. executed by burning] as a favorer of heresy and error. [26]

As the persecution intensified, the spread of the Wycliffe

movement was greatly hindered in England. But his teachings and his writings were carried to Bohemia (the region known as the Czech Republic today) by students who had studied under Wycliffe at Oxford. There they were embraced by John Hus and his followers. Thus, the torch was passed to Europe where Hus and Luther and others took up the cause of reforming the Christian church.

After forty-one years of rest in his sepulcher, Wickliffe's enemies ungraved him and turned him from earth to ashes; which ashes they also took and threw into the river. And so was he resolved into three elements, earth, fire, and water, thinking thereby utterly to extinguish and abolish both the name and doctrine of Wickliffe forever. But these and all others must know that, as there is no counsel against the Lord, so there is no keeping down of verity, but it will spring up and come out of dust and ashes, as appeared right well in this man; for though they dug up his body, burned his bones, and drowned his ashes, yet the Word of God and the truth of his doctrine, with the fruit and success thereof, they could not burn.[27]

The Avon to the Severn runs,
And Severn to the sea;
And Wycliffe's dust shall spread abroad
Wide as the waters be.[28]

MARTIN LUTHER

3

The Reformers

In the 1400-1500s the world was ripe for cataclysmic change. The clergy had become a class unto themselves—totally secularized, seeking power, pleasure, and wealth.

> Ritual increased. Preacher gave way to priest, the Lord's table to the altar, the apostle to the pope. Excommunication turned into execution. The Latin Bible was known only to priest and monk, and even then it was little studied. Without the Bible, apostasy went unchecked while ordinary people fed on superstition and fear. [29]

Simultaneously the decline of the Dark Ages gave way to scholasticism, humanism, and the period known as the Renaissance. New concepts were embraced. Music and art flour-

ished. Intellectual curiosity led to what is called classical education. Scholars began to explore new subjects which led to an interest in studying original Greek texts including the New Testament.

Into this unprecedented time of change came Johann
Gutenberg with his great gift to the world, the moveable type
printing press which revolutionized the spread of information
and knowledge. No longer would books have to be created one
at a time, painstakingly hand copied. Now written materials
could be mass-produced. Setting up shop in Mainz, Germany,
in 1450, Gutenberg was contracted to produce 200 copies of the
Latin Bible on rag (cotton) paper. Each page consisted of two
columns with 42 lines of print and each book totaled 1,282 pages. Needless to say, the process was costly. Additionally, he was
to create 30 books on vellum made of calf skin, which was even
more expensive. Out of money, Johann was forced to acquire
a partner—a lawyer named Johann Fust. Using the tools of his
trade as security against the funds advanced by his partner proved
to be tragic as the inventor/printer was never able to repay the
money borrowed. Being a lawyer, Fust did what lawyers do: he
sued Gutenberg, won the case, and ownership of the entire publishing venture. Though Gutenberg died in poverty and obscu-
rity, today his invention is credited with closing the door on the
"Dark Ages."

With this, all the pieces were in place for something to
happen.

The story of the Reformation and the courage of the men
who turned the world upside down and changed the church forever are thrilling indeed. I would love to include a complete and
total accounting of this era and mention each and every one of
the key figures in this historic drama, just as John Foxe did in his
Book of Martyrs. However, since it is my intent to limit the scope
of this book to those who undertook the translation of the Word

of God, you'll find that the brief biographies in this chapter represent only a few vital pieces of the Reformation chronicle.

Erasmus

DESIDERIUS ERASMUS ROTERODAMUS was born the illegitimate son of a monk. At age eleven, the plague struck first his mother and then his father. Those appointed to care for him also succumbed to the plague within several years' time. It has been told that often the religious orders, looking toward future recruitment into their cloister, preyed upon vulnerable children, and virtually kidnapped them. Faced with the prospect of being homeless and penniless, young Erasmus had little choice but to seek shelter in an Augustinian monastery. There is little doubt it was his experience among the monks that made him their determined enemy the rest of his life.

Erasmus had the temperament of a free spirit. And though he despised the rigors and restrictions of monastic life, with his sharp mind and keen wit, he excelled as a scholar. At length, the Bishop of Cambrai saw potential in the young man and sent him to study at the University of Paris where he was warmly welcomed by the intelligentsia. Next, he was given the opportunity to study Greek at Oxford where he made the acquaintance of John Colet and Thomas More which led to a lifelong friendship between the men. On every occasion, Erasmus dazzled and amazed those of reputation, including Pope Julius II whom he met on a visit to Rome. "The pope asked him to stay and write papers [for him], but he declined, considering Rome another tempting cage in which he would end up with his wings clipped."[30]

Erasmus owed much of his popularity to his provocative writings. His *Manual of the Christian Soldier* exposed the irrelevance of many of the church's rituals as well as its dogma. The satire *In Praise of Folly* portrayed those in authority—both princes and popes, and in particularly the monks that he despised—as being pawns to foolishness.

In 1516 he produced the greatest, most enduring work of his lifetime. Desiderius Erasmus collected the ancient Greek manuscripts of the entire New Testament. He compiled and printed them with a Latin translation alongside it. Consisting of 672 pages, this was the very first time the New Testament was made generally available in the original language. This edition formed the basis for the translations that were to follow throughout Europe.

As the Reformation fires were kindled, Erasmus was viewed as the man in the middle. He saw the abuses and errors in the Catholic Church. He spoke about them in his writings and in his lectures. Clearly, he was not an ally to the church, though he remained part of it throughout his life. But to Luther and the other reformers, he never quite went far enough. Still, his influence was obvious.

> From the very beginning of the momentous events sparked by Martin Luther's challenge to papal authority, Erasmus' clerical foes blamed him for inspiring Luther, just as some of Luther's admirers in Germany found that he merely proclaimed boldly what Erasmus had been hinting.[31]

Indeed, Erasmus said of himself, "I laid the egg which Luther hatched."

Martin Luther

"As SOON AS the coin in the coffer rings, the soul from Purgatory springs." This was the advertising jingle of Dominican friar Johannes Tetzel, one of Germany's most successful indulgence merchants. In fact, whenever he or one of his cohorts entered a town a procession ensued. The parade consisted of the papal charter approving the sale—complete with the Pope's seal—carried on a satin cloth. This would be followed in order by the priests, monks, town officials, schoolmaster, pupils, and then the town's people singing a tune together and waving flags and banners. Bells were rung in the church as the procession arrived announcing that the sale was to commence.

Wittenberg, Germany, on the date of October 31, 1517, had an even more carnival-like atmosphere. It was All Saints feast day and pilgrims from near and far had converged not just to celebrate the holy day as they did every year, but also to take advantage of the unique opportunity to view a magnificent collection of saints' relics on display at Castle Church. It had been advertised that indulgences would be granted on the spot to any and all who viewed them.

It was in this environment that Augustinian monk Martin Luther chose to post his "Ninety-five Theses" to the church door. The large document printed in a small font, outlined his arguments against the Catholic Church's unbiblical dogmas—including the proclamation that salvation could be purchased or earned through good deeds. The peasants who passed by the article were mostly illiterate, so the controversial challenges were of no value to them, except to arouse their curiosity. But Luther's intention was primarily to provoke public discourse of these issues which he sincerely hoped would cause biblical reasoning to prevail. For this reason, he simultaneously mailed copies of his theses to Archbishop Albrecht, the most important churchman in all of Germany, as well as to Luther's immediate superior, the bishop of Brandenburg.

> . . . more than posting of the theses in a backwater like Wittenberg, these letters were the provocation that ensured a response. One of Luther's talents, evident even then, was his ability to stage an event, to do something

> spectacular that would get him noticed . . . Whatever
> really happened on October 31, 1517, there is no
> doubt of the significance of the theses themselves: The
> Reformation truly was sparked by a single text.[32]

The five hundredth anniversary of the posting of the Ninety-five Theses was celebrated worldwide a few years ago. Numerous books were published and articles written commemorating the Reformation superstar. One modern-day biographer has claimed that "we know more about [Luther] than any other sixteenth century individual, allowing us to trace his relationships with his friends and colleagues through his own correspondence."[33] Luther's own collection of works totals more than 120 volumes. Add to that the biography compiled by his personal friend and fellow reformer Philip Melanchthon, and we have a very thorough picture of his entire life.

In brief, Martin Luther was born November 10, 1483, in the German village of Eisleben. He was educated at the University of Erfurt, earning his MA at the age of twenty-two, after which he began lecturing in ethics and philosophy. Persuaded by his parents, he intended to pursue a career in civil law when a catastrophic event occurred. On that day, Luther was walking in the woods when a violent thunderstorm overtook him. He sought shelter beneath a large oak which, unfortunately, was struck by lightning. John Foxe recounts that the bolt forced the terrified young man to the ground, but instantly killed a companion nearby.[34] This near-death experience caused a deep spiritual awakening within young Martin. His response was to withdraw from worldly pursuits and take up residence at an Augustinian monastery where he devoted himself to reading the works of theologians.

> . . . but in turning over the leaves of the library, he ac-
> cidently found a copy of the Latin Bible which he had

never seen before. This raised his curiosity to a high degree. He read it over very greedily and was amazed to find what a small portion of the Scripture was repeated to the people [by the priests].[35]

Soon after taking his priest's orders, he was sent to the University of Wittenberg where he became a professor of biblical literature. Martin Luther's love for the Word of God continued to grow. Through prayer and continual study he became zealously convinced that man is freely justified by God only through faith. In order to better equip himself to proclaim this doctrine and to earnestly lecture his pupils on the Epistle to the Romans, Luther applied himself to the study of Greek and Hebrew.

The more he studied, the clearer it became to the scholar and professor that the "new" things he was learning were in sharp contrast to the Catholic Church's claims. Especially distressing was the church's assertion that it possessed the power and authority to grant salvation or a lessening of suffering in the afterlife to those who were able to contribute to the church's growing wealth. If God bestowed salvation as a free gift accessed by faith in Jesus Christ, then the church's teachings were certainly an abomination to God. This provoked him to the historic actions of All Saints Day 1517.

A few years later, Pope Leo X issued a Bull (a binding decree) requiring Luther to recant under threat of being excommunicated for his supposed heresy. He was given sixty days to respond. At the time, the political climate was rife with tension as Germany's princes and the emperor himself resented the authority that Rome claimed over their sovereign land. Because of this it was arranged that Luther's case be heard in Germany instead of appearing before church hierarchy in Rome. Thus, he was ordered to appear before a council in Worms, (known as the Diet of Worms).

Luther began his trip to Worms on April 2, 1521. The journey to the Imperial Diet did not embody the repentance the church had hoped for. The journey to Worms was more like a victory march; Luther was welcomed enthusiastically in all of the towns he went through. He preached in Erfurt, Gotha and Eisenach. He arrived in Worms on April 16 and was also cheered and welcomed by the people.[36]

As the hearing commenced there was great expectation on the part of both friends and foes. The hall was standing room only. In attendance were the accusers from Rome as well as notable German princes and Emperor Charles. The nobles and the Emperor had not only come for official business but also to see and hear for themselves the great and famous Martin Luther.

What transpired during the two day session was a bit of an anticlimax. On a bench before which Luther stood was a large pile of his books and articles. The titles were read aloud and the accused was asked to give a yes or no answer to two questions: Are these your books? Do you wish to renounce them?

Luther took advantage of this illustrious audience and had a clear, clever, and well thought out answer prepared. Among his entourage of supporters there were also scribes who kept a verbatim account of what was said, lest his words be twisted against him. Far from a one word answer, his speech concluded thus:

Therefore, Your Most Serene Majesty and Your Lordships, since they seek a simple reply, I will give one that is without horns or teeth, and in this fashion: I believe in neither pope nor councils alone; for it is perfectly well established that they have frequently erred, as well as contradicted themselves. Unless I shall be convinced by the testimony of the Scriptures or by clear reason, I must be bound by those Scriptures which have been brought forward by me; yes, my conscience has been taken captive by these words of God. I cannot revoke anything, nor do I wish to; since to go against one's conscience is neither safe nor right: here I stand, I cannot do otherwise. God help me. Amen.[37]

At the conclusion of his presentation Luther felt exhilarated and victorious, though in reality his fate was sealed. His response had infuriated both the Pope and the Emperor and a few days after the Diet concluded an edict was signed which declared him a stubborn, schismatic, and public heretic. No one was to shelter him, nor feed him, nor buy, sell, possess, or read any of his printed works. However, the Emperor did grant the outlaw safe passage back to Wittenberg.

Knowing it was under just such a "safe passage" the early reformer John Hus had been arrested and subsequently burned at the stake, a few of Luther's influential supporters waited until he had begun his journey home and then staged a kidnapping. The famous monk was then disguised as a knight and sequestered in a remote castle in the woods near Eisenach.

Here, out of the limelight for the first time in many years, the pen of Martin Luther was very active. He wrote letters and theological treatises. But when it became apparent he would be stuck in Wartburg Castle indefinitely, the former monk began his most important work: translating the Bible into German. He was not the first. There were other fifteenth and sixteenth century German Bibles; but Luther's work was set apart.

In under eleven weeks, he translated the entire New Testament from the original Greek, not from the Vulgate . . . It was a work of genius. Luther's New Testament reshaped German language itself, as Luther's German became dominant, unifying what had been a wide range of local dialects . . . but what sets Luther's translation

> apart is his sense of the music of rhythms of everyday
> speech. . . . This is a Bible designed to be read aloud and
> to be heard by ordinary people. [38]

Ten years later, his work on the Old Testament translated directly from the Hebrew was also completed. Here was the means to guarantee the reforms God had begun through the pen and preaching of Martin Luther would have lasting impact. As he had always exhorted his supporters and detractors to examine church doctrine and theology by the Word of God, at last that vital, life-giving tool could be in the hands of everyone whether priest, noble, or peasant.

Unfortunately, Luther spent the remainder of his days in less noble pursuits (in the author's opinion). He developed a structure for his newly formed church, solidified his doctrines, and established a catechism to which those who preached in his name should adhere. Lutheranism was born. And in some ways, it began to resemble the hierarchy that he had opposed in the Catholic Church.

Seasoned by years of battling the powers in Rome, Luther turned his assault on those within the movement. He began devoting time and energy to disputing doctrine with other reformers with whom he was once allied. His letter writing and pamphleteering was passionate and personal. Filled with name-calling and accusations that his former friends were "spawn of the devil," he strayed far from his previous appeal that all doctrinal discussions be conducted civilly and based strictly on Scripture.

So much venom. So much hatred. Sadly, it is so in the church today. Scripture-twisting is common and heresy and compromise are the hallmark of many local churches in the name of ecumenism. Consequently, contending for the faith, once, for all, delivered to the saints is a heroic and necessary calling. However, we would do well to remember to always, "speak the truth in love." Let's be aware that God is concerned with our character as well as our doctrine, and seek to please Him in everything.

Luther and Erasmus

MARTIN LUTHER AND Desiderius Erasmus argued over free will. Erasmus promoted man's free will to the extent that he viewed it as man cooperating with God in man's own salvation—that with his God-given free will man was able to consider and choose the right way. Luther held that free will died with Adam and Eve and, in total depravity, man cannot choose. Thus, salvation comes to us by God's grace alone, with man making no contribution in the matter.

> Eventually, Erasmus's disagreements with Luther became an open rupture. In 1524, Erasmus wrote a reasoned defense of the role of free will in salvation. He defended free will against Luther's doctrine of justification by grace through faith and its implicit belief in predestination. Without free will, Erasmus argued, human moral action would not have any meaning. Luther responded with his treatise "On the Bondage of the Will."[39]

Clearly these two scholastic giants passionately held opposing views on the topic of free will. In reality both views are supported by Scripture. This might be disturbing to many believers who desire to reconcile the supposed contradiction.

One evening I was at Calvary Chapel in Costa Mesa, California, and I was waiting with a number of others for the chance to ask my pastor Chuck Smith for some scriptural clarification on a topic which I cannot recall today. As I stood nearby, I overheard a young man ask Chuck about this question of free will. Pastor Chuck's answer was simple and clear. "The way I see it," he said, "when we are entering into heaven, we will approach an archway and the banner on the top will read, 'Whosoever will may come.' Then when we have passed through, if we were to turn back and observe that same banner from the other side, it would read, 'You have not chosen Me, but I have chosen you.'" Both of these scriptural facts are true, though it may be difficult or impossible for our human minds to fully grasp. This is by God's design.

Luther and Zwingli

THE TOPIC OF COMMUNION caused a great split among the leaders of the Reformation. Luther held a position known as "consubstantiation", that is, Christ is present in the bread and wine, even though the bread and wine remain unchanged. He went so far as to say that if Christ's presence in the elements were a physical reality, He was present regardless of the faith or attitude of the recipient. In comparison, the Catholic doctrine that the Host or Eucharist and the chalice of wine or juice are mystically changed into the literal body and blood of Christ after the elements are consecrated by a priest is known as transubstantiation. Consubstantiation refers to the belief that Christ's presence co-exists alongside or in the bread and wine when Communion is received.

Other leaders in the Reformation Movement, whom Luther called sacramentalists, opposed Luther's view of consubstantiation. Ulrich Zwingli, the Swiss reformer, believed that since Christ's body had ascended into heaven it could not be present in the bread of the Lord's Supper. The view that partaking of the communion elements was a symbolic act as Christ commanded, "Do this in remembrance of Me" was endorsed by Zwingli and many others. This became the mainline position in Protestantism. Zwingli and Luther broke fellowship over this issue alone. This grieved Zwingli greatly.

Ulrich Zwingli had built his large following in Zurich on his love for systematically teaching the Word of God. The people admired him for his selfless service to those who had fallen ill from the plague even though he himself was also stricken. The preacher drew the ire of Rome for his criticism of any and all religious practices not endorsed by Scripture, such as saint worship, celibacy for the priesthood, indulgences, and the display of graven images. Nevertheless, Zwingli continued to promote infant baptism and, in fact, severely persecuted the Anabaptists who opposed this view.

> It is important to point out that those who led the Reformation were not infallible individuals. They were grieved by the way Christianity had departed from Scripture and had a desire to make corrections. But some of their corrections were not biblically based. How tragic it is today that many sheep follow these men (even naming themselves after them) and their ideas more than they follow the Lord Jesus Christ and His Word. Even though a correction to the course of Christianity was made, the corrections often did not go far enough, or in some cases veered away from biblical truth altogether. In other cases, some reformers did not want to leave the Catholic Church but rather desired to change *some* things but leave other beliefs that were just as detrimental intact. Nevertheless, many of these men and women suffered greatly for their efforts to stand for truth.[40]

What began as a unified evangelical awakening had become splintered as leaders vehemently defended their own theological territory. Despite the disagreements and infighting a lot was still accomplished which brought the true gospel of God forward in the world. As the focus of this book is on guardians of the

Word—those who translated the Bible into the languages of the people—I want to summarize this chapter by highlighting those accomplishments. Erasmus compiled the Old Testament manuscripts in Hebrew and the New Testament manuscripts in Greek and had them published alongside the Latin. Martin Luther produced a common dialect German Bible. Ulrich Zwingli provided the leadership for a group of scholars to translate the Zurich Bible, a Swiss-German edition.

"Infinite potentates have raged against this book [the Bible], and sought to destroy and uproot it . . . they nothing prevailed; they are all gone and vanished, while the book remains and will remain forever . . . Who has thus helped it—who has thus protected it against such mighty forces? No one, surely, but God Himself, who is the master of all things. And 'tis no small miracle how God has so long preserved and protected this book; for the devil and the world are sore against it."
—Martin Luther. Table talk[41]

4

William Tyndale

Fugitive, Translator, Martyr

O f all the heroes I have studied in preparation for writing this book, William Tyndale is the most inspirational to me. Others argued doctrine and church errors—Tyndale did also. But his single passion was to get the Holy Word of God into the hands of the common people. He offered many concessions in his attempts to see this dream realized (apart from compromising the Scripture itself). He was certainly brave, single-minded, focused on the task at hand. His greatest fault was that he was naïve in taking people at their word which left him open to betrayal.

The records of William Tyndale's birth are muddied by the

change of surname. Born near the Welsh border in Gloucestershire, England, as William Hychyns (Hitchins) in 1494, his family subsequently changed their name to Tyndale and vacated the family estate. It is presumed this was caused by the social difficulties that arose upon the conclusion of the War of the Roses.

We can pick up the telling of his biography with young William's studies at the renowned Magdalen Hall in Oxford. Enrolled there from 1506 to 1515, he looked forward to pursuing theological studies in earnest. However, Tyndale soon discovered that under the authority of the church, the required curriculum actually locked him out of the study of the Holy Scriptures, which he loved, and instead forced upon him the learning of the errant teachings of the Catholic Church. Making the most of his time at Magdalen and later at Cambridge, he began focusing his scholastic endeavors outside the college walls on the study of multiple languages; mastering French, German, Italian, Spanish, and—important to his life's calling—Latin, Greek and Hebrew. During this time Tyndale realized just how sheltered the lay-people were from hearing the truth of God's Word. The priests fed their parishioners only the tiniest morsels from the Scriptures which they themselves scarcely understood.

> Many English priests were so ill-educated that Tyndale claimed that twenty thousand of them could not have translated into English the line from the Paternoster: "fiat voluntas tua sicut in coelo et in terra," "Thy will be done in earth as it is in heaven."[42]

In 1521, Tyndale accepted a humble position as tutor to the children of Sir John Walsh near the city of Bristol. The Walshes were a godly family and the quiet environment suited William well. He spent his private evening hours in his small attic room practicing his translation skills by rendering small portions of

Scripture and useful Christian articles from Latin into English.

> Tyndale translated into English a work by Erasmus
> called the Manual of the Christian Soldier. This little
> book, written in 1502, described the spiritual armour
> of the Christian Knight, and the rules by which he
> should order his life. Erasmus urged the reader to ap-
> ply to study the Scriptures and the book abounded in
> quotations from the Word of God. Tyndale courteously
> presented a copy of his translation to [his hosts] and
> they were clearly proud of their tutor's scholarship and
> impressed by his serious and gracious way of life.[43]

William also enjoyed the open exchange of theological ideas
that took place among the various prestigious guests the Walshes
frequently invited to share their meals.

> In the late spring or early summer of 1523, Tyndale
> first mentioned his plan to translate the Bible. He was
> disputing with a "certain divine, reputed for a learned
> man." At one stage in their argument, Foxe wrote, the
> divine said: "We were better off to be without God's
> laws than the pope's." Tyndale blazed with godly zeal
> at this blasphemy—"God's laws" meant the scriptures,
> and "the pope's" meant canon law—and he replied that
> he defied the pope and all his laws. "If God spare my
> life," he added, "ere many years I wyl cause a boye that
> dryveth the plough shall know more of the scripture
> than thou doest."[44]

Such exchanges grieved Tyndale deeply. The life-giving,
soul-strengthening Word of God which could lead all men to
salvation should be available for anyone and everyone to read and
understand. But translating the Scriptures was a dangerous occu-
pation. No doubt he was well aware that just two years before,

seven people had been burned at the stake for teaching children to recite the Lord's Prayer in English in opposition to the 1408 law against Wycliffe's Lollards. Though compelled to be an instrument of God in accomplishing this worthy task, Tyndale possessed a peaceful nature. He did not wish to stir up strife unnecessarily, so he sought a way to proceed without breaking the law of the land and thus endangering his gracious hosts, the Walsh family.

> Tyndale was the scholar of action. In fact, Tyndale's decision was not necessarily unlawful. After Wycliffe and his Lollards an act was passed prohibiting any man from translating the Scriptures without the authority of a bishop. In theory, at least, Tyndale required only an episcopal patron. Bishop Tunstall of London was a fine scholar . . . and highly recommended by Erasmus. In his simplicity Tyndale reasoned that the opposition of the country clerics was largely because of their gross ignorance; he had only to present himself and his credentials to a man of learning and he could continue to work without further hindrance. His only purpose was to settle in London and translate the New Testament to enable the common man to read it for himself.[45]

Much to Tyndale's surprise and dismay, not only did Bishop Tunstall decline his support, but he officially opposed this proposal altogether.

> Tyndale came quickly and sadly to the conclusion that there was nowhere in England he could safely translate the Scriptures, and, when translated, nowhere to print them. There was only one course open. Accordingly, sometime in 1524 Tyndale broke the law of England and slipped away to the continent without the king's consent.[46]

Life on the Continent (How a Fox Feels)

TYNDALE'S MOVEMENTS ON the continent are somewhat difficult to trace chronologically and this is by design. Now an outlaw in the eyes of his countrymen, he seems to have anticipated that the bishop and the king would send out spies to apprehend and return him to England to face charges. It is believed he went by the name of Dalton at least part of the time—mixing up the syllables of his last name.

WILLIAM TYNDALE

He wore disguises when he traveled about and the fact that he was fluent in numerous languages allowed him to pose as a traveler of various national origins. Wittenberg, Hamburg, Marburg, Cologne, and Antwerp, Belgium—he lived in poverty as a fox on the run, subsisting on nothing but the kindness of friends as he managed to evade the hounds baying at his heels. And yes, there were spies crisscrossing the land, offering rewards for any information leading to Tyndale's capture.

As for the work itself, it is remarkable how quickly it progressed. Within ten months Tyndale had completed the translation of the New Testament. This displays that the hand of God was with him, for he had no one to consult for individual word choices (except for Englishman William Roy who assisted at the conclusion of the project). Plus, he accomplished this monumental task while on the run, carting with him the texts he was translating from as well as his notes and completed manuscripts.

> In his translation work Tyndale showed . . . independence of mind. He had no English translation beside him, not even a handwritten copy of Wycliffe's Bible; . . . It is certain that Tyndale had Luther's New Testament before him on his desk and in addition he could make use of Jerome's Latin Vulgate, the Bible of the medieval church. But the latter was in many places inaccurate and nowhere did Tyndale repeat its errors. Apart from these two, Tyndale may have possessed no other text than Erasmus's Greek New Testament which he used with great ability. In all his translation Tyndale reveals a scholarly refusal to be cast into the mould of Luther or Jerome ... but again and again he strikes out boldly on this own, a slave to no one.[47]

During the time of Tyndale's translation efforts, the written English language was still in its infancy and it was common for people to read aloud, even to themselves. This may be part of the reason Tyndale's words sound so right when spoken from the pulpit. He had an ear for the language. His colorful vocabulary allowed him to select just the right word in each passage. Indeed, it can be noted that Tyndale did much to shape the English language itself. The phrases in Tyndale's Bible even impact our speech to this day.

> Tyndale succeeded in his great aim; his language and style broke free from the stilted medieval scholastic approach. Tyndale's New Testament was earthy, almost rustic and certainly plain enough for the ploughman. He made the Bible what God intended it to be: a book for the people.[48]

The New Testament complete, William Tyndale added an introduction to the front of book:

> Give diligence dear Reder (I exhorte the) that thou
> come with a pure mynde and as the Scripture sayeth
> with a single eye unto the words of health and of eternal
> lyfe: by the which (if we repent and believe them) we are
> borne a newe, created a fresshe and enjoye the frutes off
> the bloud of Christ.[49]

And the search for a printer began. With the spies always a few steps behind, there were several close calls as the operations were discovered and broken up just as the job was beginning. Finally Tyndale found success in the city of Worms with a printer willing to take the risk. The first copies of Tyndale's New Testament were smuggled into England in 1526.

The smuggling operation itself is an amazing story of God's providence. An underground network developed between the German steelyard merchants and the English longshoremen. The New Testaments were concealed in shipping containers with an identifying mark affixed. Remarkably at this time England was suffering the effects of a famine, the corn and grain crops having failed. Germany saw this as a magnificent trade opportunity and the shipments of grain leaving German shores heading for London greatly increased. This decreased the likelihood of spiritual contraband being discovered by the king's overworked inspectors.

> But with the cargoes of grain another seed was smuggled
> in, a seed more precious and more necessary to England
> than all the wheat in the world . If the German Steelyard
> merchants rescued England from famine of corn, they
> certainly provided also that the Bread of Life which
> would satisfy the nation's spiritual hunger.[50]

> For the first time in the long history of the nation, a
> printed English New Testament was available for those
> who could afford to pay one shilling and eightpence for
> an unbound copy . . . wherever a poor man or woman
> could be found able to read, a few would club together
> and buy a copy of the Scriptures. The price was relative-
> ly cheap, probably not more than half a week's wages for
> a labourer . . .[51]

William Tyndale's dream became a reality: the Bible in the
hands of the common people in words they could understand—
words of life that would transform their hearts and their nation.

Hounds on the Hunt

IT WAS INEVITABLE with so many copies of the Holy Book flood-
ing into England that Bishop Tunstall would eventually come
upon a copy himself. Holding it in his hands and recognizing it
as the work of William Tyndale, the bishop became enraged and
immediately mandated all copies be seized and burnt and that
smugglers and booksellers be subjected to excommunication or
worse. An emergency meeting of bishops was convened so there
would be unanimity in quelling this threat. As a justification for
his ire, Tunstall proclaimed to Thomas More and the others that
Tyndale's edition was full of heresy and that he himself had found
more than three thousand translation errors.

But it is a fact that even by scholarly examination today,
Tyndale's translation work is considered impeccable. So, the
question needs to be asked, if this translation was so critically
recognized as the work of careful scholarship, why then did the
Catholic authorities render it heresy?

> There is really only one answer to this. The Scriptures in
> English would allow every man, even the ploughman, to

test the church, its doctrines and practice, for himself. And that would be disastrous. But the Church leaders could hardly admit this, so other reasons were found.[52]

And so Tyndale was accused of willfully distorting the text to suit his own views. In reality, what it comes down to is that the bishops particularly disdained the rendering of a few simple words. Tyndale had dropped certain words in preference of new ones that avoided the implications of Rome's false teaching. For example, the words, *penance, charity, priest,* and *church* were replaced with *repentance, love, elder,* and *congregation.* The church's use of these terms did not agree with what the Scriptures meant by them and Tyndale's replacements set the words free from their traditional interpretations.

Raids were made at book markets and private homes. Bibles were gathered and publicly burned in huge bonfires. When word reached Tyndale in Germany, he was shocked that his enemies would go to such lengths to prohibit something that was so obviously beneficial to the nation.

> Tyndale mocked the fact that his Testament was illegal. Who could be "so despiteful that he would envy any man so necessary a thing" as the scripture in English. Who was so "bedlam mad" enough to deny them the gospels in their own tongue.[53]

Thomas More countered the mocking tone with vitriol of his own. It was not the Holy Bible that was being destroyed but a dangerous impostor.

> More said that "no good Christian manne hauing any drop of witte in his head" should marvel that the New Testament had been burnt, for it had not. What had been consumed in the fire at St Paul's Cross was

Tyndale's Testament, "for so hadde Tyndall after Luthers counsayl corrupted and changed it from the good and wholesome doctrine of Christ to the devilishe heresyes of their own, that it was cleane a contrarye thing." Tyndale was "a hellhound in the kennel of the devil . . . discharging a filthy foam of blasphemies out of his brutish beastly mouth." The words were as "full of errors as the sea is of water," More said and much of it was "willfully mistranslated . . . to deceive blind unlearned people."[54]

As a result bounties were increased in an attempt to persuade even Tyndale's friends to betray his whereabouts. Once again the Lord protected Tyndale and he managed to be one step ahead of his accusers. There is record of only one actual encounter with a spy and this account shows what lengths Tyndale was willing to go to so the Word of God might become available throughout England. An envoy named Stephen Vaughan was sent by King Henry VIII to try to persuade the renegade translator to return to England. Vaughan caught up with Tyndale in Antwerp, Belgium, and delivered the message he was sent to convey in the name of the king. Tyndale's response, which was carried verbatim back to the king, conveys the single-mindedness of his ultimate objective, as well as the wisdom and discernment given to him by the Lord.

If it would stand with the king's most gracious pleasure to grant only a bare text of the scripture to be put forth among his people, like as is put froth among the subjects of the emperor in these parts, and of other Christian princes, be it of the translation of what person soever shall please his majesty, I shall immediately make faithful promise never to write more, nor abide two days in these parts after the same: but immediately to repair unto his realm, and there must humbly submit what

> pain or torture, yea, what death his grace will, so this be
> obtained. And till that time, I will abide the asperity of
> all chances, whatsoever shall come, and endure my life
> in as many pains as it is able to bear and suffer.[55]

He thus offered never to write again, to return to England, to submit himself to torture and death at the king's pleasure. William Tyndale would comply with all this if only the Bible — in whoever's translation the king chose, and in "plain text" without glosses or notes —could be given in English to the people. With this, the fox slipped away once more.

Old Testament

MEANWHILE, BEFORE THE hounds could pick up the trail again, William fixed his attention on the translation of the Old Testament. Though Tyndale had a remarkable grasp of many languages, his understanding of Hebrew has been described as mind-boggling. It is assumed there were, by this time, Hebrew grammars and dictionaries at his disposal, yet the Bible scholar was self-taught in every respect. It would seem that performing vital translation work in this manner, all on your own with no experts to consult with, would be a tedious daily chore. Tyndale did not find it so. He loved the whole Word of God and found being immersed in the writings of Moses refreshing. He fell in love with the Hebrew language and found that it lent itself to English more readily than to Latin.

> The properties of the Hebrew tongue agreeth a thousand
> times more with English than with Latin. The manner
> of speaking is both one, so that in a thousand places
> thou needest not but to translate into English word for
> word.[56]

Upon completing the Book of Deuteronomy William Tyndale declared: "This is a book worthy to be read day and night and never to be out of hands. [It is] a very pure gospel."[57] By 1530 the first printed copies of the Pentateuch reached English shores bearing the bold inscription: W. T. to the reader.

Betrayal

IN 1535 WILLIAM Tyndale's kind-hearted naiveté contributed to his undoing. A charming young man wheedled his way into Tyndale's circle of acquaintances in Antwerp. Soon a friendship developed between the two. Henry Phillips presented himself as a prosperous man of the world and a student of his new-found faith. In reality, he was in deep financial trouble as he had stolen money from his own father to cover a gambling debt. It is suggested that he was enticed to set up a scenario for betrayal by the lucrative reward for the capture of the notorious outlaw William Tyndale.

As the two friends were leaving the house to dine together one evening, Phillips stepped back to allow Tyndale to precede him through the door. Two men were waiting. They seized Tyndale and he was taken to Vilvoorde Castle, near Brussels. It was the end. Tyndale never left.[58]

The situation in the castle dungeon was dire. Cold. Dark. Lonely. The only visitors permitted were those sent to pressure him into renouncing his work and his beliefs. Several of Tyndale's close friends petitioned for his release but to no avail. Still, by what little light that penetrated his dark cell in the daylight hours, Tyndale attempted to continue writing articles and advancing his Old Testament translation.

After eighteen months the long-awaited trial began. A formidable list of charges was drawn up against him. Among them — that faith alone justifies; belief that the forgiveness of sins and embracing the mercy in the gospel was enough for salvation; denial of purgatory; and that neither the virgin nor the saints could be invoked to intercede.

For the trial, William Tyndale rejected the offer to obtain counsel. He knew a solicitor would want to defend him over the charges at hand. He did not wish to defend himself in this manner. Instead he wanted to use his final opportunity to defend his Bible. He testified:

> I call God to record, against the day we shall appear before our Lord Jesus, to give a reckoning of our doings, that I never altered one syllable of God's Word against my conscience, nor would this day, if all that is in the earth, whether it be pleasure, honour or riches, might be given me.[59]

The verdict was a foregone conclusion; he was condemned as a heretic. A few days later the pageant for casting him out of the church commenced in the town square. William Tyndale was led out in his priestly robes in front of dignitaries and onlookers. He was ceremoniously stripped of his official garments, had his dead shaved, and returned to his cell.

Death

IN OCTOBER OF 1536, his sentence was carried out. Early in the morning when the sun had barely risen he was brought from the dungeon to an open place near the city gate. People jostled for a better view as the prisoner was led to the stake and given one last chance to recant.

> A silence fell over the crowd as they watched the lean form and thin, tired face of the prisoner; his lips moved with a final impassionate prayer that echoed round the

stillness of that place of execution and reached to God who controls the counsels of men: "Lord, open the King of England's eyes!"[60]

William Tyndale was moved into place. His feet were bound to the stake and an iron chain was fastened around his neck with a hemp noose at his throat. The executioner stepped behind him and yanked the noose with all his force. In a moment he was strangled to death. Then the pile of brush and logs surrounding the stake were ignited. As the flames rose, the body fell limp. William Tyndale passed to his reward at the age of forty-two.

Legacy

Tyndale's legacy is, in many ways, greater than any of the other translators and reformers of his time. He was a humble man with a single quest.

> Tyndale declared his desire never to cause strife over opinions, never to gain a personal following and never to translate for any other motive than to lead men to faith in Christ and to a holy life in consequence. He was eminently successful in each area. Tyndale's mind was too large to become engrossed in the details of secondary matters or embroiled in the ensuring battles; similarly, though men talked of the Lutherans and Zwinglians, the word Tyndalians can be found only once in contemporary writings and it was evidently soon dropped as being wholly inaccurate. But more than anywhere Tyndale was successful in leading men to faith in Christ, and all England owed a heavy debt to the man who gave it the Gospel in the English New Testament.[61]

The enemy managed to strangle Tyndale's voice. He caused this martyr's body to be burned. He incited the enemies of the gospel to seize and burn every English Bible they could find. But the devil's efforts to squelch the work of William Tyndale failed utterly. His words and work live on today.

1 Corinthians 13 – Tyndale's Translation

Though I speake with the tonges of men and angels
and yet had no love
I were even as soundynge brasse:
and as a tynklynge Cynball.
And though I coulde prophesy and vnderstode
all secretes and all knowledge:
Yee if I had all faith
so that I coulde move mountayns
oute of there places
and yet had no love I were nothynge.
And though I bestowed all my gooddes
to fede the poore
and though I gave my body even that I burned
and yet have no love
it profeteth my nothynge.

KING JAMES

5

The King James Version

An English Bible Becomes Authorized

He stood almost alone among Englishmen when the king, the bishops and all Europe threw their weight against him. Within a few years of his death, the king, the bishops and all Europe were beginning to awaken to the need of the Scriptures in English. **It is not that Tyndale's translation, under the cloak of Coverdale and Rogers, was accepted because times were changing. On the contrary, it was Tyndale's translation that *was* changing the times and thus the whole course of English history. William Tyndale *was* the Reformation in England.**[62]

L ord, open the king of England's eyes." It was only one year after William Tyndale prayed this earnest final prayer that God moved to fulfill this request.

The political climate of England was fluctuating rapidly. King Henry VIII seems to have always been in the midst of controversy. Detesting the authority that Rome held over his personal life, he extended some sympathy toward the reformers. Some of those loyal to William Tyndale endeavored to take advantage of this situation.

Miles Coverdale sought to submit his own Bible translation (which reflected much of Tyndale's work) for Henry's approval. He even dedicated it to the king and to "his dearest wife, and most virtuous princess, Queen Anne."[63] Official sanction was denied.

Next to attempt this feat was the honorable John Rogers. Rogers came into contact with Tyndale in Antwerp and the deep friendship that developed was providential. After the publication of the Pentateuch in English, William continued to work on the translation of the Old Testament. For safe keeping, the fox on the run had left his unfinished manuscripts in John Rogers's possession. It is unclear by whose hand the balance of the Old Testament was completed. It is possible Rogers and Coverdale collaborated on this.

Nonetheless, by 1537, (just one year after Tyndale's execution) the completed Bible was delivered to England in hopes of securing permission to publish. The manuscript was taken by courier and given to Archbishop Thomas Cramner. The archbishop asked Thomas Cromwell (Henry VIII's chief advisor) to present it to the king. The permission sought was to be merely a temporary concession until a "better" translation could be produced by the bishops. "This," Cramner had suggested, "would occur one day after doomsday." Rogers had used the pen name

Thomas Matthew as the creator of this Bible to disguise the work of the discredited Tyndale. However, at the end of the Book of Malachi, Rogers had inserted in very large type the tell-tale initials W. T. Remarkably as King Henry VIII thumbed through the copy before him, he must have skipped that page. He pondered the political advantages to authorizing, at last, an English translation of the Holy Bible, and quickly gave his approval.

The Matthew Bible (as it was called) did not remain in circulation for long but it paved the way for subsequent revisions. One such revision made without the anti-Catholic commentary the Matthew edition contained, was made available directly to the public instead of only through the church. In addition, a royal declaration commanded it be displayed in every church in the land. The churches provided a reading desk and chained the huge book to it. This ornate volume became known as the Great Bible or the Chained Bible. "Bible reading, which had once been forbidden, then silently tolerated, then licenced, was now commanded, and for this we are indebted to Thomas Cromwell"[64] and to Miles Coverdale, John Rogers, and of course, W. T. himself.

Changing Monarchs

THE RAPID AND drama-filled succession of English monarchs caused the winds of religious intolerance to blow first one way and then the other. The blame for this can probably be placed at the feet of Henry VIII, for he was both unpredictable and temperamental, marrying, divorcing, and beheading his wives at will. The king desired to divorce his first wife, Catherine of Aragon, because she had been unable to provide him with a male heir. The pope would not allow this and Henry responded by establishing the Church of England, with himself as the head of the church.

Several wives and a few female offspring later, Henry finally attained a male heir in Edward VI. Henry VIII reigned from

1509-1547. Upon his death, son Edward began ruling at the age of nine. Naturally, as a child, the boy relied upon his advisors for rulings, policies, and opinions. It just so happened the counsellors who most readily had his ear favored the reformers over the pope. And so, during his tenure as monarch he made further changes in the Church of England with the goal of retaining Protestantism after his reign had ended. And indeed his reign was short. Young King Edward VI was stricken with tuberculosis and succumbed in 1553 at the age of fifteen.

He was succeeded by his half-sister Mary, daughter of Henry's first wife Catherine. And then everything changed. John Foxe in his *Book of Martyrs* introduces the reign of "Bloody Mary" this way:

> The circumstances of England evolved thusly: Under the reign of the young monarch Edward VI, the cause of the Protestants was greatly promoted and the gospel had a less hindered course for the space of six years. Upon young Edward's untimely demise Mary usurped the throne and revived the authority of the pope which had lain dormant.
>
> Mary was crowned at Westminster in the usual form and speedily commenced the execution of her avowed intention of eradicating and burning every Protestant. Her elevation was the signal for the commencement of the bloody persecution which followed.[65]

Whatever her motive for unleashing such fury on those who held opposing religious views, Mary was relentlessly cruel in carrying out her objective. The new queen's very first victim was none other than the architect of the Matthew Bible, John Rogers. Though many other reformers had fled the continent in anticipation of what was to come, Rogers had remained, determined to pursue the gospel changes his nation needed. Arrested after preaching at St. Paul's Cathedral, he was burnt at the stake in 1555. A fellow prisoner commented on this first martyr of Queen Mary I: "He [Rogers] broke the ice quite valiantly."

Mary died of cancer in 1558 ending her bloody reign. Because she had no children, her half-sister Elizabeth, daughter of Anne Boleyn came into power.

ELIZABETH FACED CHALLENGES from the beginning of her reign— all of a religious nature. Catholics wanted to retain Catholic rule in England. Many influential families welcomed this idea. Second—many Protestants who had fled during Mary's reign flooded back home, bringing with them the reformed theology they had acquired from John Calvin in Geneva. These returnees were at odds with Church of England practices, including the wearing of clerical vestments and the obligatory use of the Book of Common Prayer. But the chief complaint had to do with church government. The Church of England was led by the monarch with bishops appointed by him or her. Calvinist beliefs placed the church over the state. These ideas were incompatible, and Elizabeth felt this was a threat to her power. In addition, Calvinist teachings began to permeate the universities where the clergymen were trained.

Also the smaller less expensive Geneva Bible translation was the edition that people were using in their homes. The notes and comments contained therein reflected Calvinistic theology as well as blatant anti-monarch sentiments. The reform movement gained ground. Adherents were called Puritans.

In 1570 Elizabeth was excommunicated by Pope Pius V who then called upon British Catholics to resist her authority. A plan by the Jesuits to assassinate the queen was discovered and thwarted. This called for drastic measures. Elizabeth imposed an oath of allegiance for all known Catholics and others who were considered disloyal. Catholics were not only denied religious freedom but also ordinary rights as citizens. In the end, two hundred Catholics—clergy, laymen, women—were executed for refusing to take the oath or under other "treasonous" charges.

Radical Puritans also entered the fray, opposing the queen and rejecting her bishops. Some of them also refused the oath of loyalty and were subsequently imprisoned.

Meanwhile in Europe, the Counter-Reformation was in play. Those countries deemed Catholic nations were growing in power and world influence (chiefly Spain and France). There was concern that British shores might be invaded by such entities in retaliation for Elizabeth's actions against her Catholic citizens.

> But by the end of Elizabeth's long reign, the most serious religious tensions within England no longer had anything to do with those between Protestants and Catholics. The new battles concerned two different styles of English Protestantism —Anglicanism [Church of England] and Puritanism.[66]

Queen Elizabeth had managed to suppress the growing hostilities between the Anglicans and the Puritans—chiefly by ignoring the rift. But what would happen after her demise? Enter the peacemaker . . .

King James (1566-1625)

ELIZABETH DIED IN 1603 with no offspring. After searching through the family tree to find a suitable replacement to the throne of England, it became obvious King James IV of Scotland was the only obvious viable candidate.

He was male, Protestant, and possessed both rank and experience of government. James had a strong hereditary claim to the English throne, and already had children—so the question of who would succeed James would not be as difficult as in the case of the childless Elizabeth.[67]

This was welcome news for the English Puritans. They were envious of the inroads Calvinism had made in Scotland. They believed the hour had come at last to set up a proper Protestant nation in which the compromises of the Church of England would be done away with. So great were their hopes and ambitions that even while James was journeying south from Scotland for his coronation, a delegation of Puritans intercepted the soon-to-be king and presented him with a petition outlining their demands for reform.

Their hopes were decidedly misplaced. In reality the new king despised the Puritan presbyterian form of government. He opposed their Geneva Bible as well, which included notes dispelling the "divine right of kings" which James strongly adhered to.

> The simple fact of the matter is that James had not the slightest intention of promoting a Puritan or Presbyterian agenda in England. He thoroughly detested what he had seen in Scotland, and did not wish to encounter the same difficulties in England. He much preferred the Anglican system of church government, seeing the institution of episcopacy as a safeguard to the monarchy.
>
> English Puritans, who were not aware of James's strong views on this matter, naturally assumed that they were about to receive a monarch who would not merely take them seriously, but would actually be sympathetic to their agenda. It would take some time before the real state of affairs became clear—and James made the most

of that window of opportunity to neutralize the Puritan threat, while pretending to honor its concerns.[68]

Needless to say, the bishops were alarmed when they learned their opponents had gotten a head start in approaching the new king. But James already had a plan. Soon after taking the throne, he convened a conference which was to be attended by him, the council, various bishops, and other learned men to deal with these religious disputes.

The notes that have survived from the Hampton Court Conference show King James the peacemaker in action. The conference itself was heavily stacked in favor of the Church of England. There were nineteen bishops and only four moderate Puritans who had been hand-picked. James began with a long speech establishing the king's God-given right to formulate and endorse religious policies and practices. He then permitted the Puritan delegation to state their case for reform. Primarily, they requested the liberty to conduct their worship services as dictated by the Bible as opposed to the current requirement that the Common Book of Prayer be used. James diplomatically rejected this request.

> This left James in a somewhat unpromising position. Wanting to be seen to be conciliatory and pacific, he was finding himself unable to offer any sops to his Puritan subjects. Everything pointed to his ending up endorsing something remarkably close to the status quo, which would please the bishops and alienate the Puritans. A gesture was clearly needed, unless the conference was to be perceived as totally one-sided. The Puritans needed to propose something to which he could readily assent. Given that the bishops seemed to oppose virtually everything the Puritans were requesting, he would find himself in conflict with the Church of England in doing

so. Yet being a king was about give and take. He had defended the Prayer Book, he could give way on something else.[69]

But what could that be?

A solution presented itself when the leader of the Puritan group suggested the Geneva Bible be named the authentic Bible to be used in church services instead of the currently approved Bishop's Bible. Probably realizing this would be strongly opposed, another Puritan suggested that any number of translations could be used in any given church.

James saw his opening. There should be but one Bible for all of England. He declared that since he had yet to see a Bible "well translated into English" the time had come to try again. Plans for a new, superior English Bible were underway.

The King James Version

THE HAMPTON COURT Conference came out with this resolution:

> A translation be made of the whole Bible, as consonant as can be to the original Hebrew and Greek; and this to be set out and printed, without any marginal notes, and only to be used in all churches of England in time of divine service.[70]

James directed that the entire text of the Bible (including the Apocrypha) be divided up into six sections and assigned to teams of translators who were selected for their fine scholarship and knowledge of Greek and Hebrew, as well as Latin. The translators were to number no more than fifty-four, and both Anglicans and Puritans were represented. The work was to take place (two teams each) at the universities in Oxford, Cambridge, and Westminster.

As each team completed a section of Scripture, they were to

submit it to the other teams for review. Notes and suggestions of changes to the text were compiled and corrections made where needed.

Richard Bancroft, the bishop of London, drew up the strict rules for translation which were to be stringently followed. James approved these stipulations. Among the rules:

> The ordinary Bible read in the Church, commonly called the Bishops' Bible, to be followed, and as little altered as the Truth of the original will permit.

> The names of the Prophets, and the Holy Writers, with the other Names of the Text, to be retained, as nigh as may be, according as they were vulgarly used.

> The Old Ecclesiastical Words to be kept, viz. the Word Church not to be translated Congregation, etc.

> When a Word hath divers Significations, that to be kept which hath been most commonly used by most of the Ancient Fathers, being agreeable to the Propriety of the Place, and the Analogy of the Faith.

> No Marginal Notes at all to be affixed, but only for the explanation of the Hebrew or Greek words, which cannot without some circumlocution, so briefly and fitly be expressed in the Text.

> These translations to be used when they agree better with the Text than the Bishops' Bible: Tindoll's, Matthew's, Coverdale's, Whitchurch's, Geneva.[71]

The King James translators were well aware they were standing on the shoulders of giants, as these rules reflect. Those translators who had gone before them had blazed a trail they were, no doubt, proud to follow. They believed the alterations to the text which they found necessary to make, would have been approved by their predecessors. The corrections were not based merely on whim, but on better scholarship in the languages that had since become available. Thus, the King James Bible cannot be dismissed as simply a revision of previous translations. Accuracy and readability were the primary goals.

This can be established by the preface inserted in the finished manuscript.

> The Translators to the Reader. Truly (Good Christian Reader) we never thought from the beginning that we should need to make a new Translation, nor yet to make of a bad one a good one, . . . but to make a good one better, or out of many good ones, one principal good one, not justly to be excepted against; that hath been our endeavour, that our mark.[72]

Impact

THE COMPLETED 1611 edition of the King James Version of the Holy Bible did not gain immediate acceptance. Scholars were critical of the numerous typographical errors. Some pointed out that quite a number of the words carried over from earlier translations were already archaic by this time. Bishops retained a sense of loyalty to the previously authorized Bishops' Bible. And common folk still preferred the smaller and more affordable Geneva Bible with which they were familiar.

Acceptance came gradually. Eventually it became heralded for the fine piece of scholarship it truly is. The translators took great care in selecting the best possible English word equivalent for each individual context. Instead of rendering a particular Greek word the same in every instance, attention was paid to how the word was used. As the translators themselves put it:

> . . . there be some words that be not the same sense
> everywhere—we were especially careful, and made a
> conscience, according to our duty. But, that we should
> express the same notion in the same particular word; as
> for example, if we translate the Hebrew or Greek word
> once by PURPOSE, never to call it INTENT; if one
> JOURNEYING, never TRAVELING . . . if one where
> JOY, never GLADNESS, etc. . . . For is the kingdom of
> God to become words or syllables? Why should we be
> in bondage to them if we may be free, use one precisely
> when we may use another no less fit, as commodiously?[73]

The prosaic and poetic elegance which resulted was a sort of
happy accident. In seeking to enhance the readability of the text,
the committees inadvertently produced what has been recognized
as the greatest piece of English literature of all time. In fact, the
King James Bible (along with the works of William Shakespeare)
has been credited with stabilizing the previously fluid English
language. Rules of spelling and grammar began to be adhered
to uniformly as opposed to the free-for-all approach of previous
generations. This was truly a milestone in the development of the
English language as a whole.

The King James Version has certainly stood the test of time.
Even today it ranks second in the list of best-selling Bible translations in the United States. It is rated as the most often read Bible
version in America by a margin of two to one over the next most
popular New International Version.

Bishops' Bible

IN 1564, DURING the reign of Queen Elizabeth, Archbishop
Matthew Parker set about to create a revision of the Great Bible
with the hope of weakening the popularity of the Geneva Bible.
He assembled a committee of qualified clergymen and divided

the Bible into segments for them to complete. In many ways, the guidelines set forth were similar to those given to the translators of the King James Bible in the decades to come. The scholars were to omit any commentary and to consult previous translations, adhering to them as much as possible. Unfortunately, the work of the various translators reflected each man's individual style and nobody bothered to make the complete manuscript cohesive. The finished product contained a number of woodcuts and maps which rendered it a costly book to produce. The Bishops' Bible never received official acceptance and is generally considered to be the weakest of all the Bibles from that era.

The entirety of Your Word is truth,
And every one of Your righteous judgments
endures forever.
Psalm 119:160

Psalm 23 Comparison

Matthew Bible (1537)— The Lord is my shepherde, I can want nothynge. He fedeth me in a grene pasture, & ledeth me to fresh eater. He quickeneth my soule . . .

Great Bible (1539)— The Lorde is my shepherd, therefore can I lack nothing. He shall fede me in a grene pasture & leade me forth beside the waters of comforte. He shall conuerte my soule . . .

Geneva Bible (1560)— The Lord is my shepherd, I shal not want. He maketh me to rest in grene pasture, & leadeth me by the stil waters. He restoreth my soule . . .

Bishops' Bible (1568)— God is my sheephearde, therefore I can lacke nothing: he wyll cause me to repose my selfe in pasture full of grasse, and he wyll leade me vnto calme waters. He wyll conuert my soule . . .

King James Bible (1611)— the LORD is my shepheard, I shall not want. He maketh me to lie downe in greene pastures: he leadeth mee beside the still waters. He restoreth my soule . . .

DEVELOPMENT OF THE ENGLISH BIBLE
1350 A.D.—1610 A.D.

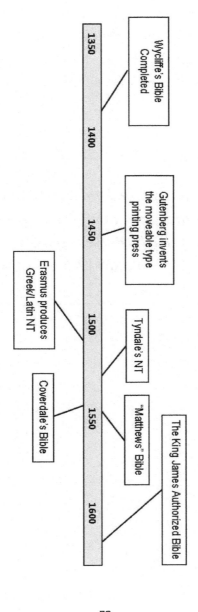

1350	1400	1450	1500	1550	1600

Wycliffe's Bible Completed

Gutenberg invents the moveable type printing press

Erasmus produces Greek/Latin NT

Tyndale's NT

"Matthews" Bible

Coverdale's Bible

The King James Authorized Bible

The words of the Lord are pure words,
Like silver tried in a furnace of earth,
Purified seven times.
Psalm 12:6

6

The Art of Translation

Walk into any Christian bookstore and peruse the many shelves of Bibles and it's easy to become confused. Different translations or paraphrased Bibles have been created for various reading levels. There are Bibles labeled for women, men, teens, children, soldiers, recovering addicts, and various ethnicities. Some contain notes and commentaries, and some do not. Why so many? Which should you choose?

Among Bible-readers there is often discussion about which Bible translation is "best" or most accurate. Sometimes, unfortunately, these discussions can turn into heated arguments and even church splits; this is not a good thing. Colossians 4:6 says, "*Let* your speech always *be* with grace, seasoned with salt, that you may know how you ought to answer each one." The difference of opinion comes down to the translation philosophy of the translator and also which of the available manuscripts were used as the primary basis for the text. This chapter is not meant to sway anyone away from their firmly held conclusion, nor is it my intention to promote one method or translation above another. The objective here is to examine the art of translation itself.

Manuscripts

IT IS INTERESTING THAT there is very little controversy over the Old Testament Hebrew text. We have documented the diligence of the Jewish scribes and the careful preservation of the scrolls. Regrettably, the same cannot be said for the New Testament Greek manuscripts. There are basically two schools of thought in this debate—those who accept what is known as *Textus Receptus* as the most authoritative, and those who acknowledge the validity of the codices discovered in the nineteenth century. Here is a simplified—let me emphasize: *simplified* —look at the pros and cons of both positions.

The letters and Gospels handwritten by the apostles to the churches had been copied and recopied on papyrus, and then circulated far and wide, with editions landing in the major population centers of the world. *Textus Receptus* or Received Text is the name given to the collection of Greek manuscripts of Scripture used by Christians in certain population centers of the Greek-speaking world for many centuries. Said to be universally read and accepted by the early church, these were compiled and published together as one volume by Erasmus in 1516. This version was used by Luther and the other reformers for their translation work. The King James Bible was based on these texts. Additional proof for their veracity is that when compared with early writings of various leaders from the onset of Christianity, over 86,000 verses were found and these matched perfectly with the Received Text.[74]

Some argue that *Textus Receptus* had been corrupted over the years at the hands of errant or misguided copyists. Additionally, because Emperor Constantine essentially legalized and encouraged Christianity in his realm (Byzantium or modern-day Turkey) circa 350 AD, larger numbers of this edition were produced as compared to copies originating from other parts of the world. This is why *Textus Receptus* is also known as The Majority Text. Critics say that just because there are more of them does not mean they are the most accurate.[75]

The manuscript controversy did not start until the late nineteenth century. The discovery of *Codex Sinaiticus* and *Codex Vaticanus* were heralded as the oldest or earliest New Testament manuscripts in existence. The thought is that since these were less far removed from the original writings, they were less likely to contain copy errors or deliberate alterations. These were not written upon papyrus but rather on animal skins and bound together in books. This is what the term *codex* refers to. They are estimated to date back to the fourth century. In 1881 Brook Foss Wescott and Fenton Hort published *The New Testament in the Original Greek* which relied primarily but not exclusively upon *Codex Sinaiticus* and *Codex Vaticanus*. Known simply as Wescott and Hort, this publication is used as the basis for just about all of the modern Bible translations today.

Detractors claim neither of these codices is complete—that is, containing the full canon of Scripture. *Vaticanus* contains the Apocrypha and ends at the Book of Hebrews. What remains of *Sinaitcus* is only one-half of the New Testament and it also contains some additional books that are not from the New Testament or even from the Apocrypha. Each of these contains a number of discrepancies from the Received Text and in fact disagree with one another in more than 3,000 instances in the Gospels alone. Besides, in this century new discoveries of even older papyrus fragments have been discovered—eighteen from the second century and even one from the first century—and these agree with *Textus* Receptus in over 90% of instances.[76]

So . . . which of the many available New Testament manuscripts is the most reliable? This is a question Bible translators must answer according to their own conviction.

Either way, the reliability of the Bibles we have today should not be in question. It is to God's glory that today there are over 5,500 Greek manuscripts or fragments known to be in existence—and this number is increasing yearly as new discoveries are made. Compare this with other ancient writings which are still being translated and read today. Only 190 manuscripts of Homer's *Iliad* have survived and only 7 manuscripts exist of *The Works of Plato* (and these 7 are 1,000 years removed from Plato's pen). Yet there are never discussions in literatures courses about whether or not the English editions of these classics are accurate.

> Readers may be assured that textual debate does not affect one in a thousand words of the Greek New Testament. Furthermore, no established doctrine is called in question by any doubts about the correct reading in this or that text. The Christian can approach his New Testament with confidence.[77]

We can have firm assurance that God is able to preserve His Holy Word and it is still effective to change lives and lead people to salvation.

Methods

TRANSLATING THE HOLY Scriptures into any tongue other than the original requires another vital decision beyond which Hebrew and Greek manuscripts to use as the source or beginning point. There is another frequent confusion or disagreement in the discussion of which Bible translation is best, and this involves the translation philosophy that has produced the finished edition. We would hope those undertaking such a task would take it seriously and realize the importance of their work and their ultimate accountability to God, the Bible's author. However,

> The process of translating is more complicated than it appears. Some people think that all you have to do when making a translation is to define each word and string together all the individual word meanings. This assumes that the source language (in this case, Greek or Hebrew) and the receptor language (such as English) are exactly alike. If life could only be so easy! In fact, no two languages are exactly alike.[78]

So, how do you get the words to line up so that they actually make sense to the reader of a receptor language? There are three major philosophies or methods that are used to achieve this, each with its own set of pros and cons. There is the literal or word-for-word translation, the dynamic equivalent or thought-for thought version, and then there is the paraphrase. Let's investigate the attributes of each mode.

The Word-for-Word translation is not literally a literal translation as it is often named. Scholars doing translation work from scratch would most likely begin by building an interlinear Bible as a study tool. This would consist of the original language text (Hebrew, Aramaic, Greek) written word for word alongside literal English (or other receptor language) words. This would cause a rendering of John 2:4 to read like this:

> And says to her the Jesus what to me and to you woman not yet is come the hour of time.

As you can plainly see this is practically useless for one's daily devotions!

Instead, in creating a word-for-word translation of Scripture, a translator will attempt to stay as close as possible to the original word choices, word order, and style of writing that were inspired by God when the author wrote them. Only if using a literally equivalent word would obscure the writer's obvious meaning, is another word choice selected. Next, the scholar would apply proper rules of grammar to the sentence so that it makes sense in the receptor language. This puts an emphasis on accuracy while at the same time making the text understandable to a modern reader. While this may require the student of a word-for-word Bible to put in some extra effort to uncover the significance of cultural references or idiomatic renderings, the result is a more well-rounded, better-informed Christian.

> Even though it is impossible to follow the word order of the original in an English translation, the translator will attempt to stay as close as possible to the effective and persuasive use that the style of the original language permits. In other words, what is stated in the original language is rendered into English, as well as the way that it is said, as far as possible. This is why the literal translation is known as a "formal equivalence."[79]

The **Dynamic Equivalent** or Functional Equivalent translation seeks to render the Scriptures on a thought-by-thought basis. That is, the translator attempts to discern what the original writer meant by what he said. He or she then puts down that thought in an easy-to-read or conversational style of English or other target language. These editions may be suitable for those who are at a rudimentary reading level, or maybe for those who are seeking a more casual Bible-reading experience. Be aware that the translator's biases may have flavored their choices in determining what the author meant to say.

The translation known as the **paraphrase** is really not an actual translation at all. It is defined as "the restatement of a text, passage, or work, giving the meaning in another form." Instead of placing the emphasis upon accuracy to the Scriptures as God breathed them, the highest consideration for the Bible paraphrase (such as The Message) is upon the target audience—i.e., how easy it is for the common reader (typically geared toward seventh graders) to understand.

Here is a Scripture comparison of how a verse is "translated" using each of these three methods. I have chosen versions that are commonly known for each of the modes we have just identified.

	1 Corinthians 2:14
WORD FOR WORD **King James**	But the natural man receiveth not the things of the Spirit of God: for they are foolishness unto him: neither can he know them, because they are spiritually discerned
THOUGHT FOR THOUGHT **New International Reader's**	Some people don't have the Holy Spirit. They don't accept the things that come from the Spirit of God. Things like that are foolish to them. They can't understand them. In fact, such things can't be under-stood without the Spirit's help.
PARAPHRASE **The Message**	The unspiritual self, just as it is by nature, can't receive the gifts of God's Spirit. There's no capacity for them. They seem like so much silliness. Spirit can be known only by spirit - God's Spirit and our spirits in open communion.

	Ecclesiastes 9:8
WORD FOR WORD **King James**	Let thy garments be al-ways white; and let thy head lack no ointment.
THOUGHT FOR THOUGHT **New International Reader's**	Always wear white clothes to show you are happy. Anoint your head with olive oil.
PARAPHRASE **The Message**	Dress festively every morn-ing. Don't skimp on colors and scarves.

	Romans 12:2
WORD FOR WORD **King James**	And be not conformed to this world: but be ye trans-formed by the renewing of your mind, that ye may prove what is that good, and acceptable, and per-fect, will of God.
THOUGHT FOR THOUGHT **New International Reader's**	Don't live any longer the way this world lives. Let your way of thinking be completely changed. Then you will be able to test what God wants for you. And you will agree that what he wants is right. His plan is good and pleasing and perfect.
PARAPHRASE **The Message**	Don't become so well-adjusted to your culture that you fit into it without even thinking. Instead, fix your attention on God. You'll be changed from the inside out. Readily recog-nize what he wants from you, and quickly respond to it. Unlike the culture around you, always drag-ging you down to its level of im-maturity, God brings the best out of you, devel-ops well-formed maturity in you.

Additionally, you can refer to the chart below to see where your favorite Bible falls on the spectrum of methods.[80]

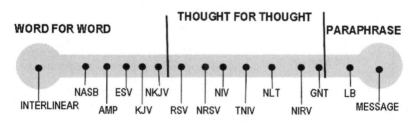

AMP-Ampified	NASB- New American Standard	NRSV-New Revised Standard
ESV-English Standard	NIRV- New International Readers	RSV-Revised Standard
GNT-Good News	NIV-New International	TNIV-Today's New International
KJV-KingJames	NKJV-New King James	
LB-Living Bible	NLT-New Living	

Some Other Challenges

FOR THE REMAINDER of this book, I want to turn the focus away from ancient languages and English translations to some of the other amazing translation work that has been done in making the Word of God available to the multitude of tongues and languages that exist in this big, diverse world. To gain a greater appreciation of the art of Bible translation let's examine some of the other difficulties each translator might encounter in his or her task.

To the missionary who is called by God to serve in some remote village, the first necessary obstacle to tackle is to learn the language. In some especially primitive areas this might involve a language that has never been committed to writing. Before the job of translating the Word of God can even begin, an alphabet must be created from scratch, as well as rules of grammar that fit the speech of the people. Then, working closely with native speakers, a dictionary or lexicon must be compiled. Next a literacy program must be established to teach the folks to read their own language. At last, the true goal of translating the Holy Scriptures can begin. Throughout this process, the missionary must rely upon willing indigenous helpers so they can have a full and complete understanding of word meanings and nuances. This process requires dedication and patience because it may be decades before even the first Gospel is completed.

Along the way, other setbacks may occur. A missionary who was just beginning his life's work of translating the Bible into the dialect of a remote tribe recounts one such obstacle. Having secured the help of a willing, young indigenous lad, the missionary began to grasp the tribal language. It took years but at last the pair succeeded in creating a written alphabet for the language. Next, they worked side-by-side to compile a dictionary for the dialect. They rejoiced when this step in the project was complete, for it was the precursor to actually beginning the Bible translation project. The celebration was short-lived however, for it was at this time that one of the tribal elders informed the translator discreetly, "You know, this lad has a speech impediment. He pronounces the words funny." The missionary had no choice but to scrap his dictionary and begin again with another assistant.

Often there is no equivalent word to substitute for a particular word of Scripture. This could be as simple as communicating with a society that contains no reference to sheep or wheat or other nouns that Jesus used in His parables. Or it could be as daunting as rendering theological "Bible words" like *sanctify* or *redemption* or *atonement*. These are huge challenges to be sure and it should come as no surprise various translators might select totally different receptor language words to convey the same concept in the Scriptures.

A tremendous amount of skill and integrity is required to successfully accomplish the art of Bible translation. Here is an example of just how terribly wrong things can turn out. This is how Psalm 23:1-2 was rendered by an inexperienced interpreter for a group of inhabitants of a seaside village in the far north of Canada:

> God is my goat hunter. I don't want him! For he flings me down on the mountainside, and drags me down to the sea.[81]

Who would want to follow a God like that?

Sometimes the culture of the people causes confusion to the message of the Scripture. The problems this can cause a translator are numerous. Jack Popjes recounts several examples of this in his book, *The Why and How of Bible Translation*.[82] Here is one example from the twenty-two years of translation work that he and his wife undertook among the Canela Indians of Brazil:

> Our Canela translation helpers were totally confused when we began to translate the story of the wise man building on a rock and the foolish man building on the sand. Canelas build their villages on packed sand or sandy soil mixed with red clay. The only rock in the area is volcanic, very sharp, and painful to walk on. They would never dream of building a house on rock. How could they dig holes in rock for house poles?
>
> We had to abandon the sand and rock metaphor. We could choose to translate more generically, "The wise man built on a safe place, far away from where the river might flood the house. The foolish man built it in the path of the flood water."
>
> Or we could switch completely to a Canela cultural metaphor . . .[83]

In the end the Popjeses chose to change the elements in the parable from rock and sand to solid red clay and loose, dry sand. You can see that difficult, careful choices must be made all along the way.

Doubtless there are countless other challenges faced daily by those who are "out in the field" bringing God's Word to people who don't yet have access to it in their "heart language." If you know of any such guardians of the Word laboring in this task today, please remember to pray for them. Remember faith comes by hearing and hearing by the Word of God and God desires that all be saved and come to the knowledge of the truth.

There is no special holy Bible language—
not Hebrew, not Greek, not Aramaic,
not even Latin or Shakespearian English.
God reveals Himself in His Word,
and He wants it translated into
all the world's languages
so everyone may know
His great love for people.[84]

7

Go Ye Therefore

And He said to them, "Go into all the world and preach
the gospel to every creature. (Mark 16:15)

Wouldn't it be easier if everyone just spoke the same language? Imagine if all the people in the whole world
throughout every generation even to this day all spoke
Greek and Hebrew. One Bible for all people for all time. Wouldn't
that be great? Well, a quick rereading of the Book of Genesis re-
minds us that long ago it *was* that way.

Now the whole earth had one language and one speech.
And it came to pass, as they journeyed from the east,
that they found a plain in the land of Shinar, and they

> dwelt there. Then they said to one another, "Come, let us make bricks and bake them thoroughly." They had brick for stone, and they had asphalt for mortar. And they said, "Come, let us build ourselves a city, and a tower whose top is in the heavens; let us make a name for ourselves, lest we be scattered abroad over the face of the whole earth." (Genesis 11:1-4)

There, at the Tower of Babel, the people, unified with one language, had a common goal: to create a man-made path to heaven. Pride and self-sufficiency led them to declare they had no need for God. Who knows what sort of evil projects would have followed if they had been permitted to continue. As a result, God stopped them from proceeding with their rebellious endeavor.

> But the Lord came down to see the city and the tower which the sons of men had built. And the Lord said, "Indeed the people [are] one and they all have one language, and this is what they begin to do; now nothing that they propose to do will be withheld from them. "Come, let Us go down and there confuse their language, that they may not understand one another's speech." So the Lord scattered them abroad from there over the face of all the earth, and they ceased building the city. Therefore its name is called Babel, because there the Lord confused the language of all the earth; and from there the Lord scattered them abroad over the face of all the earth. (Genesis 11:5-9)

The Lord's stopgap measure was to initiate multiple languages. Communication was thwarted and the tower-building society was dispersed.

Since it was God Himself who instituted the creation of multiple languages, it stands to reason the confusion which resulted did not take Him by surprise. Our gracious God did not allow the story to end there; for elsewhere in the Scripture it is clear that not only is God aware of human diversity, but His plan of redemption extends to people of every language and nation.

One place where this concern is displayed is in the mandate Jesus left for His disciples:

> Then He said to them, "These are the words which I spoke to you while I was still with you, that all things must be fulfilled which were written in the Law of Moses and the Prophets and the]Psalms concerning Me." And He opened their understanding, that they might comprehend the Scriptures. Then He said to them, "Thus it is written, and thus it was necessary for the Christ to suffer and to rise from the dead the third day, **and that repentance and remission of sins should be preached in His name to all nations, beginning at Jerusalem.** And you are witnesses of these things. Behold, I send the Promise of My Father upon you; but tarry in the city of Jerusalem until you are endued with power from on high." (Luke 24:44-49)

And when that power arrived on the Day of Pentecost the "language issue" was miraculously addressed.

> And there were dwelling in Jerusalem Jews, devout men, from every nation under heaven. And when this sound occurred, the multitude came together, and were confused, because everyone heard them speak in his own language. Then they were all amazed and marveled, saying to one another, "Look, are not all these who speak Galileans? And how [is it that] we hear, each in our own language in which we were born?" (Acts 2:5-8)

The Christian church was truly born when the Holy Spirit was poured out. As Peter and the others preached the gospel of

Jesus Christ, the number of believers exploded. They had spiritual unity. A benevolence ministry was established. Things were good. And then persecution happened. This resulted in another scattering as the disciples moved out of their former comfort zone. The "tarry in Jerusalem" directive gave way to the "be My witness in Jerusalem, Judea, Samaria and to the uttermost parts of the earth" command. The remainder of the New Testament gives us a picture of how Paul and the others began to take the message of salvation out to the uttermost parts of the world.

In the end, the Book of Revelation gives a prophetic look at a heaven that is populated with "every kindred, and tongue, and people, and nation."

> And they sang a new song, saying: "You are worthy to take the scroll, And to open its seals; For You were slain, And have redeemed us to God by Your blood Out of every tribe and tongue and people and nation . . . (Revelation 5:9)

What is God's view of human languages? Missionary Jack Popjes answers that question and explains that since God and His plan of redemption are revealed in the Holy Scriptures, translation of the Word into all the world's language is a God-given mandate for Christ's church.

> God, who invented languages and implanted them in people way back at the Tower of Babel, loves languages. All languages. There is no special holy Bible language— not Hebrew, not Greek, not Aramaic, not even Latin or Shakespearian English. God reveals Himself in His Word, and He wants it translated into all the world's languages so everyone may know His great love for people.[85]

As testimony to the fact that Jesus' followers took this directive to heart, we can refer to the chart on page 24 to see that scholarly believers had already translated the Bible into more than 500 languages by the year 500 AD. And the next 500 years saw the addition of many more.

Missionary Fervor

ENTER THE FAMOUS explorer Captain James Cook. Whereas Dutch and Spanish explorers had investigated many of the hundreds of islands in the South Pacific, their motivation was to discover the profitability of trading with the native inhabitants, i.e., what goods they had to offer. In contrast Cook had been commissioned by British Admiralty on a scientific expedition. On board the *Endeavor* in 1769 were an astronomer and a botanist, with Cook himself serving as cartographer. Maps were charted. Diaries were kept of discoveries in Tahiti, New Zealand, and the Eastern coast of Australia which had never before been seen by Europeans.

> With a temperament more ethnographic and technical than philosophical, he [Cook] is famed as being the first of the great European navigators, uninterested in the privateering bravado of Drake, and targeted instead on missions of exploration, mapping, natural history, and navigational knowledge. Whereas the Dutch had turned back when no obvious commercial profit was to be had from their Oceanic ventures, Cook carried his sponsor with him: Joseph Banks, a botanist commanding a team of naturalists and artists to record the views, with a keen interest in theorizing settlement, migration, and cultural patterns. All of this would serve the British Admiralty well, of course, and Cook provided invaluable strategic knowledge to the navy.[86]

Cook and his crew utilized the expertise of a native Tahitian, Tupaia, who taught them much about not only the sea currents, but also the various islands and their inhabitants. When the *Endeavor* and its crew returned home to England, they described the islands as "paradise" with friendly, hospitable people, and delicious, exotic fruits. The idyllic representations of Oceania captured the imaginations of Europeans and the officers of the *Endeavor* became popular dinner guests in society circles.

However, other descriptions of tribal wars among the islanders, kidnapping, cannibalism, and the brutal murder of Captain Cook on his third and final voyage to the Hawaiian Islands sparked a very dissimilar response among a different population.

> . . . since the great navigator's brutal death, the Eden ideal had worn off; the benevolent state of nature was now a fallen paradise. Here is where accounts of South Sea islanders became crucial: church groups eagerly read shocking tales of island immorality and lack of stable governments.[87]

Here was truly a people group who needed to hear the true gospel of Christ. Missionary fervor erupted. Groups of evangelically motivated Christians formed "missionary societies" either around their particular denomination or as a gathering of like-minded saints who had a spiritual burden for a specific geographic location. The goal was to intercede in prayer for the lost tribesmen and, as often happens when believers are united in prayer, the Holy Spirit began to inspire individuals to actually go out and proselytize in faraway lands.

In 1795 the London Missionary Society (LMS) was formed around public meetings with a vision to "spread the knowledge of Christ among heathen and unenlightened nations." Concerned believers gave generously and before long enough funds were collected to charter passage for thirty missionaries bound for Tahiti aboard the *Duff.*

Henry Nott (1774-1844) to Tahiti

THE VOYAGERS WERE an eclectic group of men and women—what the LMS called "godly mechanics." Only four were formally ordained. Others were carpenters, weavers, craftsmen. All were strong in the faith and ready to preach the gospel. Among them was Henry Nott, a bricklayer by trade. They landed on the Society Islands of Tahiti in 1797.

Nott and the other missionaries found it impossible to overstate the beauty of the verdant, fruitful landscape and the deep blue of the coral seas. They also could not find the words to describe the absolute depravity of its residents. As they settled into their new environment, they were shocked by just how deeply the inhabitants were entrenched in superstition and unspeakable dark customs. The Tahitians believed human sacrifice was necessary to appease their gods. When a temple was built, its roof-stakes were driven through living human sacrifices. Each of their revered carved idols brandished a weapon—a spear, an axe, a club—inspiring the tribal warriors to utterly brutalize the captives of conquered neighboring tribes. The survivors of wars wore the skins of enemies as trophies. The elderly and the invalids were sometimes buried alive. Babies were frequently murdered by their own parents, though the missionaries never came to grasp the reasoning behind this. The chiefs were pampered and spoiled at their own insistence. Thievery was a common and seemingly acceptable practice.

The king of the realm welcomed the missionaries. The newcomers were offered food and a home to dwell in. It did not take long for the ruler's motive to display itself. King Pomare was not interested in their message nor in the God they represented.

He was hoping for access to European treasures such as superior tools, cooking pots, and cloth. He requested more and more "gifts" from the Englishmen. Other tribesmen who visited the missionaries' home followed their chief's example.

The settlers began attempting to preach to the people right away. They had procured the translation services of a Swedish sailor who had made the island his own personal paradise. Unfortunately, the man's licentious lifestyle contradicted the message of the gospel, which brought grief to Nott. By God's providence, Henry Nott not only had bricklaying skills, he also had marked linguistic abilities as well. He learned the regional dialect quickly and began poring over the Greek and Hebrew texts he had brought with him. He quickly produced his favorite verse, John 3:16, in Tahitian, and in due course was able to preach a sermon entirely in his adopted language.

The seed of the Word fell on hard, stony ground and the Tahitians remained unconverted.

> The missionaries preached and prayed and did their utmost to bring King Pomare [in particular] to a saving knowledge of Christ, but he died in 1803, a savage monster to the end. From the information obtainable, Nott estimated that, during his reign of thirty years Pomare had sacrificed 2000 human victims as offerings to his idols. His son, Otu, assumed the title Pomare II. He was, if possible, more vicious and violent than his father.[88]

The missionary band endured nearly a decade of hard labor, hardships, and heartaches. Eventually, discouragement won out. Some of the original thirty returned home. Several abandoned the service of Christ and took up secular endeavors as tradesmen. One or two were murdered by those they came to save. And one went completely insane. By the beginning of the year 1810 Henry Nott was all alone. He was "troubled . . . persecuted . . . cast down . . . but not in despair," for he believed the cause of Christ would one day triumph.

This faithful servant of Christ persevered in his efforts to bring the Word of God into the Tahitian language, believing the Bible alone could break up the hard ground and allow the gospel to take root. King Pomare II himself, eager to demonstrate his superior intelligence to his subjects, helped with word choices and phrasing. As soon as one portion of Scripture was completed, Nott would print it up with the rudimentary printing tiles he possessed and distribute it as best he could.

It was twenty-two long years of such desperate, lonely labor before Henry Nott saw his first convert in these remote islands. It was none other than King Pomare II! The once-wicked king changed his ways, and with the help of his Christian mentor, began to transform the laws of the decadent land into a paradise of godly ideals. Testimony once again that—

> All Scripture is given by inspiration of God, and [is] profitable for doctrine, for reproof, for correction, for instruction in righteousness, that the man of God may be complete, thoroughly equipped for every good work. (2 Timothy 3:16-17)

Samuel Marsden (1765-1838) to New Zealand

IN RESEARCHING BRAVE missionaries who left the comforts of home for the purpose of taking the gospel to the lost in faraway lands, it was a daunting task to limit the stories I wanted to tell. I have chosen to focus only on those for whom Bible translation was a major part of their calling. William Carey and Hudson Taylor were obvious choices in the eighteenth and nineteenth century parts of the narrative. But in the case of this man, Samuel Marsden, I have wrestled with whether to include him.

In the year 1800, Marsden was a Church of England priest who was dispatched to New South Wales in Australia to serve as chief cleric for the region and chaplain to the convicts incarcerated there. It seems he had little compassion for those he was sent to minister to spiritually. It is documented that he authorized beatings for the smallest offenses, earning him the nickname "The Flogging Parson". In 1806, Marsden was the originator of the New South Wales "Female Register" which classed all women in the colony (except some widows) as either "married" or "concubine". Only marriages within the Church of England were recognized as legitimate on this list; women who married in Roman Catholic or Jewish ceremonies were automatically classed as concubines.[89]

Marsden acquired great wealth during his residency in New South Wales. Owning thousands of acres of fertile land, he developed a special hearty breed of sheep which thrived. Shrewd and successful trading of high-quality wool with London mercantilists earned him a reputation as a respected businessman on both continents. It is said that Samuel Marsden single-handedly pioneered the Australian wool industry which is still lucrative today.

In stark contrast to this tainted legacy is the fruitful work established by Marsden among the indigenous people of New Zealand. During a return voyage from England to Australia, the chaplain met and befriended a Maori chief named Ruatara. The man had been cruelly treated after being lured to England under false pretenses. He had been worked nearly to death and left to return to his native land as best he could. Marsden took him into his home in New South Wales, nursed him back to health, and devoted six months to Ruatara's Christian education. In return the friendly chief taught the chaplain the Maori dialect. He also astonished his host with horrific stories of cannibalism practiced in his tribe. Visitors to New Zealand shores were frequently killed and eaten, while some were taken as slaves only to be consumed at a later time. Together, Marsden and Ruatara began to plan and pray for the opportunity to carry the Christian message to the Maori. To this end, the chief returned to New Zealand with Marsden's promise to come as soon as he was able.

The fulfillment of this promise was delayed. Marsden could find no ship, captain, or crew willing to land on unfriendly New Zealand shores. Word had spread of the fate of the crew of *The Boyd*, the last vessel to attempt such a landing. It had happened just as Ruatara had warned. The entire crew was massacred on the beach.

Undeterred, Samuel Marsden used his own funds, purchased the ship called *The Active*, and—

> On November 19, 1814, Marsden embarked with a motley crew of Christians and savages, together with a few horses, cattle, sheep and poultry, and on December 19, landed at the Bay of Islands, close to the scene of recent bloodshed and horror. Ruatara was there to meet him. Knowing the ferocity of his people, he did his utmost to persuade his intrepid missionary friend not to land, but Marsden insisted on going ashore, saying: "It is high time to make known the glad tidings in these dark regions of sin and spiritual bondage."[90]

On Christmas Day, Samuel Marsden preached the first Christian sermon ever delivered on the island of New Zealand. A crude pulpit had been erected by Ruatara and the congregants were seated upon overturned canoes. There were between three to four hundred Maoris in attendance to hear the gospel message in their native tongue. Reverend Marsden chose as his text Luke 2:10: "I bring you glad tidings of great joy!" The new converts among the Maori captured the heart of Samuel Marsden. His diary reflects this.

> In this manner, the Gospel has been introduced into New Zealand, and I fervently pray that the glory of it may never depart from its inhabitants, till time shall be no more.[91]

And this was only the beginning. The chaplain spent the remainder of his life working to establish the kingdom of God among these former cannibals. He brought young Maori men to New South Wales for extensive Christian education. He funded the establishment and supply of missionary outposts throughout New Zealand.

Among those missionaries housed at one of the outposts were brothers Henry and William Williams who transcribed Maori into a written language and started a literacy program for old and young. The Williamses then began the arduous task of translating the Scriptures into Maori. Before Marsden's death in 1838 over five thousand copies of the New Testament were being distributed. The Scriptures (*Te Paipera Tapu*) were greatly in demand and became a treasure to the people, more prized than blankets or muskets. One missionary wrote:

> Whenever they sit down to rest, all take out their sacred Scriptures, and begin to read. I have actually been kept awake, in my bed, till after midnight, by the natives outside reading the sacred Scriptures and asking each other questions, or passing comments.[92]

Indigenous churches thrived and the Scriptures were so highly regarded that missionaries lamented with joy that they could no longer find a passage to preach on which was unfamiliar to the Maoris.

> Surely the most pleasing aspect to the Gospel's spread
> for the missionaries must have been the reports of Maori
> evangelising Maori, sharing the Gospel and promoting
> change throughout Maori society. Maori were sharing
> the message with each other, pushing against tribal con-
> flict and brokering peace.[93]

No longer warriors and cannibals, the once savage Maoris were being transformed by the Word of God—an answer to Samuel Marsden's prayer.

God uses and chooses flawed human beings to bring glory to Himself. Certainly Marsden fell short in reflecting Christlikeness in many aspects of his life. However, who knows how much time would have passed, how many souls lost for eternity, before another believer would dare to disregard the hostile threats and carry the Good News to the shores of New Zealand.

LONG BEFORE THE British established their missionary societies, the gospel was being proclaimed among the indigenous tribes of North America.

John Eliot (1604-1690) to Native Americans

JOHN ELIOT has been called "the apostle to the Indians." As he began his work among the tribes, Eliot realized the gestures and pidgin English used by merchants who wished to trade with the native inhabitants would never be adequate for preaching a sermon. With the help of a young native lad named Cockenoe, the Puritan missionary learned the Algonquian language spoken in that region of Massachusetts. The language had no alphabet, so John Eliot developed one. Then the pair began translation work.

The Ten Commandments and the Lord's Prayer were achieved first; then other Scriptures, and finally the entire Bible—*Mamusse Wunneetupanatamwe Up-Biblum God*. The entire project, from learning the language to the finished product, took Eliot thirty years. This edition was actually the first complete Bible printed in the American colonies. And though John Eliot was not the first to bring Native Americans to Jesus Christ, he was the first to provide the life-giving Scriptures to them in their own language.

David Brainerd (1718-1747) to Native Americans

DAVID BRAINERD is frequently cited by other missionaries as the one who most inspired them to begin their lives of sacrifice and service to the Lord. This is remarkable because Brainerd's ministry to the Native American tribes in Pennsylvania, New York, and New Jersey only lasted forty-three months.

Though raised in an extremely strict religious home, David himself did not make a life-changing decision to follow Christ until he was twenty-one years old. Almost at once he set his sights on becoming a pastor and enrolled in Yale College to obtain a license to preach. His plans were thwarted, first, by the onset of tuberculosis, and second by his expulsion from college over some hastily spoken words. The era was the period of revival known as The Great Awakening. Zealous preachers such as George Whitefield and Jonathan Edwards had stirred many of the students at Yale. Some of the young men identified their own professors as unspiritual when compared to the fire-and-brimstone orators they had heard. Brainerd made an offhand comment to that effect, was overheard, and summarily expelled.

Brainerd's "Plan B" was to go forth as a missionary to the many Native American tribes who had never heard the gospel of Jesus Christ. He obtained the endorsement of the Society in Scotland for the Propagating of the Christian Gospel. His first assignment was near Kaunameek, New York, in a village whose inhabitants were an offshoot of the Mohican Tribe. Almost immediately, David felt unequal to the task. He wrote in his diary:

> Appeared to myself exceeding ignorant, weak, helpless, unworthy, and altogether unequal to my work. It seemed to me I would never do any service or have any success among the Indians. My soul was weary of life; I longed for death, beyond measure. When I thought of any godly soul departed, my soul was ready to envy him his privilege, thinking, "Oh, when will my turn come!"[94]

Nevertheless, during his short tenure there, he learned enough of their language to pray and converse, though he preached with an interpreter. He started a school for the children and translated the Psalms to use as their primer.

The following year David Brainerd resettled in a strip of land in the forks of the Delaware River in Pennsylvania. He felt a great love for the Delaware Tribe and longed to see them accept the hope of salvation that he vehemently offered them on every occasion. But the ground was hard. His sense of helplessness and dependence on God led him deep into prayer. He would spend hours upon hours kneeling on the cold, leaf-strewn ground in the forest calling out to the Lord for their souls. This did wonders in lifting his melancholy soul but hasten the progression of his physical maladies.

His final and most fruitful mission station was in Crossweeksung, New Jersey. It was here that his fervent prayer labors, the earnest preaching, and the intimate one-on-one conversations with the native men and women had success at last. It was not as though Brainerd did anything different than in his previous assignments. He did not try a new tactic or preaching style. No, he merely continued to selflessly pour himself out as he always had done. But now, this time, God moved. In his diary, Brainerd records the tears of repentance that flowed from the listeners as he preached a simple gospel message. This was followed by obvious, radical changes in the lifestyles of tribesmen and women. This was truly God's Holy Spirit at work.

> August 8, 1745, the windows of heaven opened and revival fire fell on these seeking hearts. He had preached fervently and frequently, and the joy of seeing souls born into the Kingdom of God brought great joy to his heart. But his health was failing, and frequently he was very ill. He did not seek to educate the Indians into the Kingdom or reform them into the Kingdom—they were born into the Kingdom, often after violent emotional struggles. He wrote in his diary, "Here am I, Lord, send me. Send me to the ends of the earth. Send me to the rough, the savage pagans of the wilderness. Send from all that is called comfort in earth or earthly comfort. Send even to death itself if it is to be in Thy service and to promote Thy kingdom."[95]

David Brainerd died at the age of twenty-nine after enduring loneliness, hunger, illness, pain, weakness, and extreme depression throughout his missionary career. Eight times in his writings he referred to himself as "a worm." Frequently he was too weak and wracked with pain to leave his bed. More than two dozen times he wished for this own death, as in the following example.

> Lord's Day, December 6, [1745] Was so overwhelmed with dejection that I knew not how to live. I longed for death exceedingly; my soul was sunk into deep waters and the floods were ready to drown me. I was so much oppressed that my soul was in a kind of horror.[96]

The success of his ministry is a bit unremarkable: He baptized only about one hundred converts. The inspiration attributed to David Brainerd comes from the detailed diaries he kept of the highs and lows of his solitary missionary life. These were compiled and published with comments by the Reverend Jonathan Edwards of The Great Awakening fame. This collection, *The Life and Diary of David Brainerd*, has provided motivation to countless missionaries who would come after—including William Carey, Adoniram Judson, and Jim Elliot.

> It was not Brainerd's accomplishments as a missionary that influenced so many others. It was his acknowledgment of his weaknesses and his need to rely upon God that has drawn so many to his book.[97]

Today this collection of Brainerd's personal journal entries is still recommended reading for pastors, missionaries, and laymen who wish to be used by God. It is the testimony that God uses ordinary men and women—even those who suffer unspeakable hardships, obstacles, and limitations—to accomplish tasks that bring glory to Him. The key, as Brainerd discovered, is dependence on the Lord and the realization that "I can do all things through Christ who strengthens me" (Philippians 4:13).

THE BIBLE TO ALL THE WORLD

(a sampling)
600 A.D.—1900 A.D.

600	700	800	900	1000	1100	1200	1300	1400	1500	1600	1700	1800	1900

Chinese

Arabic

Russian
Slovak
Serbian
Bulgarian

Anglo-Saxon New Testament
(early roots of English)

French

Czech

Hungarian

Spanish

Algonquin

Luther's German Bible

Portuguese
Tahitian

William Carey begins translation of numerous dialects in India

Modern Russian

Burmese
Maori

Korean

Hudson Taylor begins translation of numerous dialects in China

8

William Carey

"Expect great things; attempt great things"

No collection about guardians of the Word would be complete without the retelling of the life and ministry of the great William Carey (1761-1834). Today this humble pastor and shoemaker is known as the "Father of Modern Missions." There are many thorough and inspiring books written about this hero of the faith. Included here are some highlights of the triumphs and tragedies of God's servant which resulted in the Holy Bible being translated into more than forty languages.

As a poor, young pastor in the midlands of England, William Carey struggled to feed himself. His congregation could not afford a salary, so he worked long into the night at the business of making shoes. As sole proprietor he also served as salesman, bookkeeper, and deliveryman. By day, the self-educated Carey taught the underprivileged village children the basics of an education, for which he received a small stipend. This left early morning for his own personal study of languages—Greek, Hebrew, Latin, and French. The weekends were for sermon preparation, preaching, and attending to the needs of his flock in the village of Moulton.

This environment of poverty and weariness fostered the great passions of William Carey's life. Biographies of missionaries such as David Brainerd and John Eliot (who translated the Bible into Algonquin) became his reading material. Inspired by the tales of Cook's voyages in the South Pacific and the mysterious inhabitants encountered on remote islands, the cobbler / pastor began collecting data from around the world. Carey saw beyond the statistics, for he knew that the numbers represented individual lost souls. He wondered how they would ever come to know the saving grace of the Lord. These thoughts fueled his prayers.

Visitors to his cobbler's shack described a strange sight. Hanging up above the workbench containing the tools of the trade was a crudely drawn world map constructed on pasted together leather scraps. On this map Carey had scrawled the names of the nations, their populations, and a summary of each land's inhabitants, their chief religion, and other characteristics he had gleaned from his research. Even the tiniest island was not overlooked. Indeed, it seems that the faraway islands were of particular interest to Carey. As he prayed over the people represented on his map, Carey developed a particular interest in Tahiti and dreamed of traveling there some day.

As he ruminated on these things, a theology developed which would serve as a blueprint for missions even to the present day. First and foremost was a call to prayer for the nations. Next, came an articulation of the biblical mandate for world evangelism. And finally, a plan of action needed to be implemented. The result was Carey's treatise with the lengthy title: *An Enquiry into the Obligations of Christians, to Use Means for the Conversion of the Heathens. In Which the Religious State of the Different Nations of the World, the Success of Former Undertakings, and the Practicability of Further Undertakings, Are Considered.* The book consisted of five chapters dealing with: 1) The Great Commission (evangelism reflects the very character of God Himself); 2) historical precedents from the apostles onward; 3) a world survey; 4) obstacles to missions; 5) the Christian's duty to promote the cause of missions.

The Lord provided a few like-minded ministers to encourage Carey's relentless pursuit. A benefactor paid for the printing of the book. Another patron gave him a subsidy so that he could continue to pursue language study and ease up on the shoemaking and teaching endeavors which consumed so much of his time and energy.

Carey became zealous in proclaiming God's missions mandate to everyone who would listen (and many who chose not to). His siblings and parents began to dread his lengthy prayers for the lost inhabitants of distant lands when they were together at family meals. The modest congregation Carey was shepherding in Moulton heard countless sermons on the plight of the "heathen" and the Christian's responsibility to them.

Other clergymen were put off by the young upstart. At a meeting of the Northamptonshire Association of Baptist ministers in 1786, the mediator of the meeting asked if any of the young pastors had a topic he would like to raise for discussion. When no one else responded, William Carey rose from his seat and proposed, "Whether the command given to the apostles to teach all nations was not obligatory on all succeeding ministers to the end of the world, seeing that the accompanying promise was of equal extent." The chairman's eyes opened wide in disbelief. He responded, "Young man, sit down: when God pleases to covert the heathen, He will do it without your aid or mine."[98]

Those words are attributed to Dr. John Ryland Jr., but they encapsulate the prevailing attitude toward world missions at the time. Yet the Lord was moving to change hearts; and by 1792 at the next meeting of the Northamptonshire Association of Baptist ministers, John Ryland had become one of Carey's most ardent supporters, as had famed pastor Andrew Fuller.

William Carey was now pastoring a thriving church in Leicester and was viewed as one of the up-and-coming preachers of the day. Thus, he was asked to deliver a sermon before the association.

> By all accounts Carey's discourse was animated and eloquent. The ferment of his prolonged study and passion for spreading the gospel among the heathen overseas poured into that one concentrated address. . . . The burden of the sermon came to a crescendo in a summarizing couplet, eight syllables, six words . . . "Expect great things. Attempt great things."[99]

Clearly many of the ministers in attendance were deeply touched. But the gathering proceeded with ordinary association business. As the time for adjournment approached, Carey was in a heightened state of distress. He clasped Andrew Fuller by the sleeve and implored, "Is there nothing again going to be done, sir?" The urgent plea was heeded, and plans were set in motion for the formation of the Baptist Society for Propagating the Gospel among the Heathen. At last there was a glimmer of hope that the answer to William Carey's prayers might be on the horizon.

The Call to Go

ONE SHORT YEAR later, the Baptist Society for Propagating the Gospel among the Heathen was approached by physician and preacher John Thomas. Thomas requested they send someone to assist him in his work in Bengal, India. The committee proposed William Carey be sent.

Now by this time Carey had a wife, Dorothy, who was pregnant with their fifth child. Their infant daughter had died of a fever, leaving Dorothy emotionally unstable. She refused to accompany her husband. Carey, in much agony, determined to go with only his eldest son Felix and send for the rest of his dear family in a few years.

This was only one of the hindrances to the planned mission endeavor. The Society had no money, so Carey and some of the other members did circuit preaching to raise funds. The team was able to raise the necessary capital for the voyage itself, but nothing to sustain the missionaries once they arrived.

Another huge obstacle was that anyone desiring to settle in India had to obtain permission from the East India Company, the British enterprise which controlled all trade. "By act of Parliament not ten years old, every subject of the King going to or found in the East Indies without a license from the Company, was guilty of high crime and misdemeanor, and liable to fine and imprisonment."[100] Carey, Thomas, and party were vehemently denied this permission. William Carey greatly feared making the voyage as an illegal alien only to be turned back once they reached the shore. He sought counsel from John Newton (composer of the beloved hymn *Amazing Grace*).

> "What if the company should send us home on our arrival in Bengal?" asked Carey. "Then conclude," replied Newton, "that your Lord has nothing there for you to

accomplish. But if He have, then no power on earth can hinder you."[101]

After hours of prayer and waiting on God for confirmation, Carey was unswervingly convinced that God was calling him to India. He would answer the call, no matter the cost.

There were no British vessels willing to transport passengers

WILLIAM CAREY

who did not have the proper documents in hand. As it turned out, the delays that brought frustration were actually orchestrated by the hand of God. At last the party was able to procure passage aboard a Dutch ship, the *Kron Princessa Maria*. By this time, Dorothy had given birth to a son. She relented and decided to make the trip. So there were eight missionaries who set sail for Bengal in 1793—William and Dorothy Carey, their four sons, William's sister, and John Thomas.

Tears were abundant as they said their farewells to family and friends. Pastor Carey's final service at his cherished church was especially heart-rending. The service concluded with Carey and the congregation singing the last stanza of this hymn:

And must I part with all I have,
Jesus, my Lord, for Thee?
This is my joy, since Thou hast done,
much more than this for me.
Yes, let it go: One look from Thee
will more than make amends
For all the losses I sustain,
of credits, riches, friends.[102]

It is hard for those of us living in this century to compre-
hend the difficulties of overseas travel in those days. Treacherous
seas, harsh or uncooperative weather, seasickness, pirates, all took
their toll. Sometimes illness struck. Sometimes supplies of food
or fresh water ran out. This particular journey took five months.

Carey put the time to good use. Thomas tutored him in the
Bengali language and together they began a translation of the
Book of Genesis. Thomas had already completed a draft of much
of the New Testament. Carey couldn't wait to get the Word of
God into the hands of the Bengalis. It invigorated him that he
was already beginning his "great work" of translating Scripture
into languages where they had never before been read. He realized his vision was too large for one man alone and dreamed
of having his sons become apprentices for the task. The devoted
father wrote in his diary:

> I'm very desirous that my children may pursue the same
> work; and now intend to bring up one in the study of
> Sanskrit, and another of Persian. O, may God give them
> grace to fit them for the work![103]

India at last!

WILLIAM CAREY EXPECTED great things for his new ministry on the shores of India. The entire first year (1794) instead was marked by heartaches and disappointment. Calcutta proved to be too expensive for the missionary troop to find lodging. They were near starving as they tried to find suitable accommodation in first one village and then another. Despite this, Carey and Thomas continued in the task the Lord called them to do; they preached daily on the streets and in the marketplaces. Few listened and none responded.

Then John Thomas learned there was a warrant for his arrest because of a large debt he had neglected back home. Dr. Thomas made the decision to remedy the problem and at the same time be able to earn a living and support his family by returning to the practice of medicine. He pilfered what meager funds remained in the mission budget to set himself up in business in Calcutta and obtain comfortable housing for his wife and child.

The Careys, on the other hand, were destitute and despairing. With absolutely no resources, William built a bamboo shack for his own family in swampland that no one else wanted. The land was inhabited by tigers and alligators. The conditions were unsanitary. Dorothy and two of the children suffered with dysentery. Mrs. Carey, who had been reluctant to come in the first place, was overtaken by latent mental illness. She had unpredictable bouts of violent outbursts which continued throughout the rest of her life, leaving the care of the children to her husband. This left her unable to be the helpmate that William Carey truly needed in his difficult ministry.

God is merciful and the Carey family was taken in by a non-believer in the region of Debhatta and given a small plot of land to farm. A Hindu man who also lived in that same household helped Carey with his language skills and also educated him in local customs. This allowed Carey to make progress in the translation of the Bible into Bengali.

After many moves, uncertainties, and trials, the Carey family finally achieved some stability. Carey (and also John Thomas) was offered an interesting proposition in Mudnabatty. Both were offered the opportunity to manage indigo plantations. This provided them with housing, a salary, and the legal means to stay in India. An added benefit was the entire indigo operation required only three to four months of direct supervision—this for planting, harvesting, and processing. The rest—the growing season—afforded unencumbered time to pursue "kingdom work."

When the Baptist Society for Propagating the Gospel among the Heathen learned of this arrangement, they were quick to criticize. How could William Carey forsake the calling of God for secular pursuits? No matter that the Society itself had thus far sent only a few pounds of support to sustain him in his work. No matter that Carey spent most of his salary on missionary endeavors, keeping very little for his own needs. Carey attributed this bi-vocational set-up not only as God's provision, but also as the realization of his firmly held belief that cross-cultural missionaries should also be "tent-makers" as was the apostle Paul.

Harvest Time

CAREY'S TIME AS plantation manager lasted for five years. During that time, the Lord also began to bring a spiritual harvest after years of seemingly fruitless planting and watering of the good seed of the Word of God. Now, when Carey engaged in the public preaching of the gospel, both Muslims and Hindus began to listen—sometimes as many as six hundred.

Finally in the year 1800 the first convert was won to Christ. Krishna Pal, a Hindu, demonstrated his faith by renouncing the caste he was born into and identifying himself with the Christian believers. This was a huge sign of true repentance.

> From the beginning Carey felt that the holding of caste
> was incompatible with faith in Christ. He refused to
> baptize anyone who continued to maintain caste dis-
> tinctions. The renunciation of caste was also a means to
> test the sincerity of new converts. As much as the mis-
> sionaries desired to win the lost to Christ, they steadfast-
> ly refused to lower the standard of Christian discipleship
> in order to puff up their numbers.[104]

Today, those who lack understanding of the biblical call to
discipleship, disparage William Carey and others like him for
being insensitive to the norms of various cultures. They claim
Western missionaries ruin indigenous populations by trying to
force submission to Western ways. It is true foreign workers need
to be cautious of unnecessarily imposing American or European
lifestyles upon their converts. However, true biblical standards
are timeless and universal. These need to be taught and encouraged as the hallmarks of Christian discipleship. Certainly the
Hindu caste system in which certain segments of population are
deemed sub-human and forever subservient to the upper classes,
is abhorrent to God. This is the case for slavery as well, which
Carey also opposed.

The year 1800 also brought the printing and distribution of
the Gospel of Matthew in the Bengali language. These became
invaluable tools in evangelism and the number of converts mul-
tiplied. Along with the increase in believers came the need for
a greater number of laborers for the harvest. God supplied this
as well. Carey led his team to Serampore on the west bank of
the Hooghly River, where they built a compound with room for
expansion. The dream was to have a facility and staff for publishing the Scriptures in various languages as the translation projects

were completed. A school for the children of missionaries was a must, but this could be extended to provide education for village children and women as well. Naturally, abundant opportunities should exist for Christian fellowship and Bible instruction. All these dreams were realized in short order.

By 1801 the first edition of the complete Bengali New Testament was rolling off the press in Serampore. For this, Carey had labored seven and a half years. What cause for rejoicing for William Carey as well as all the new believers who were anxiously awaiting their very own copy of God's holy Word. Two thousand of these "evangelists" went out to remote areas of India where missionaries had not yet ventured.

> One of the copies of this first edition made its way to the distant city of Dacca. When missionaries finally established a work there some 17 years later, they discovered several villages of Hindu peasants who had abandoned worship of idols. They were waiting for a teacher who would explain to them the faith they had learned from the frayed pages of a little book preserved in a wooden box in one of their villages. The book was Carey's Bengali New Testament.[105]

This was just the beginning. Carey's horizons regarding Bible translation were unlimited. He wrote to the Society back home:

> We have it in our power, if our means would be for it, in the space of about fifteen years to have the Word of God translated and printed in all the languages of the East. Our situation is such as to furnish us with the best assistance from the natives of the different countries . . . On this great work we have fixed our eyes. Whether God will enable us to accomplish it, or any considerable part of it, is uncertain.[106]

Andrew Fuller and the others thought this scheme too ambitious, but Carey was undaunted. Expect great things; attempt great things. Carey was following his own advice, and God had a plan to make Carey's attempts prosper. The former cobbler was offered a professorship at the prestigious Fort William College in Calcutta. Baffled at the proposal because he himself had no formal education, Carey hesitated. He sought counsel from his colleagues at the Serampore compound and as they prayed together, they felt the Lord's leading.

Professor Carey took to his new role with enthusiasm and was soon given the responsibility of teaching not only the Bengali language but Sanskrit and Marathi as well. As he divided his time between Calcutta and Serampore, the benefits of this new position became clear. First, his salary was substantial. Maintaining his own modest living expenses, he single-handedly became the primary financial support for nearly all the missionary efforts stemming from the Serampore base. This once again raised the criticism from home about the undertaking of secular enterprise.

As it turned out, the scholarly labors of the college richly complemented Carey's translation work. He had access to all the texts he could get his hands on. In addition, as senior research professor he had his own team of scholars who possessed native knowledge of Indian dialects. He put them to work as translation assistants.

Still, with all this prestige at the Fort William College, Carey's crowning work in the educational field came with the founding of Serampore College. It was clear English missionaries alone would never be able to evangelize all of India. Indigenous workers from every walk of life needed to be trained. This school was open to all, regardless of "caste" or color. It was a first-class divinity school as well as a liberal arts college, preparing the pupils for self-sustaining service to the Lord. Out of this school, came evangelists, pastors, teachers, and yes, Bible translators.

Carey's Legacy

BY THE TIME of William Carey's death in 1834, everything was in place for the work which he had begun, and which had started so slowly, to self-perpetuate. The three roots of Carey's plan to evangelize India were in place: Preach the gospel, translate the Bible, and establish schools. Proclamation, translation, education.[107]

Proclamation—From the Serampore base, Carey's team members (both British and Indian) spread throughout India. In this, William Carey was a pioneer in cross-cultural communication. He had not just studied the languages but the cultures as well. Realizing that male missionaries would never have access to female hearers in either the Hindu or the Muslim culture, Carey encouraged the cultivation of "Bible women" who could break through the gender barriers to win women to Christ. The equipping and sending of native preachers and evangelists led to the establishment of new and thriving churches in areas where Western missionaries could never venture.

Translation—Translations of the Holy Scriptures came off the printing press at Serampore in more than forty languages and dialects. Of these, Carey himself was responsible for converting the entire Bible into Bengali, Ooriya, Marathi, Hinki, Assamese, and Sanskrit. He completed portions in twenty-nine other languages. The rest (of the forty) were translated by the scholars he himself had trained (which included two of his sons). Truly a remarkable feat for this guardian of the Word.

Education—As early as 1817, Baptist workers under Carey's direction had already opened more than one hundred mission schools with sixty-seven hundred pupils attending. The teachers provided general education subjects: reading, writing, mathematics, and science to both boys and girls (which was unheard of at the time). Along with this, the children received instruction in the Scriptures as well as practical skills which could help them earn a living. For those students who felt the call of God, there was, of course, the Serampore College, for further equipping for the work of the ministry.

Serampore College is the second oldest educational institute in India, and it is still functioning today. Its website [https://www.seramporecollege.org/] boasts of its two hundredth anniversary in 2018 and states the college is still following the aim and purpose of the founders, imparting quality education in Christian Theology as well as secular degrees in Arts, Sciences, and Commerce. If you are ever in that locale, you might want to visit the William Carey Library and Research Centre which is a popular attraction to visitors. The Serampore College website entices visitors with these features:

> The Carey Library and Research Centre preserve rare papers, documents and manuscripts from the days of the founders of the college. This is a storehouse of valuable work in Oriental and European languages and holds a good number of ancient precious manuscripts. The Carey Library and Research Centre, which has the Carey Museum within itself, has become the main attraction of many academicians and research scholars from all over the world.

Shoemaker, botantist, translator, preacher, factory manager—William Carey was all those things and more. Most importantly, he was a faithful witness to the gospel of Jesus Christ amidst a life of personal grief, professional ridicule, and international strife.[108]

Today, William Carey is known as the father of modern missions. "His example proved missions work was possible; his zeal convinced people missions work was essential; and generations of missionaries [have] followed in his footsteps."[109]

Forever, O Lord, Your word is settled in heaven.
Psalm 119:89

So then faith comes by hearing,
and hearing by the word of God.
Romans 10:17

ADONIRAM JUDSON

ANN JUDSON

9

To All the World

Judson, Moffat, Crowther

Adoniram and Ann Judson (1788-1850) to Burma

A pillow, a dungeon, and a hidden treasure. These are the elements of the remarkable story of how the Word of God came to Burma (modern day Myanmar).

Though he was an American, young missionary Adoniram Judson was abducted from his home in the capital city of Ava and thrown into a Burmese dungeon as a British spy. The conditions were deplorable, almost beyond description. The room was pitch black and windowless. The stench was suffocating. Fifty other prisoners, many of whom were Brits who had been rounded up under the same suspicions, inhabited the cell. Adoniram found that his cellmates were near starvation as he would soon be. He and the others were bound by the ankles with heavy shackles. Each night, a long bamboo pole was inserted into the shackles and the prisoners' feet were hoisted into the air until each man dangled with only his head and shoulders resting on the filthy ground. Throughout the long, painful, terrifying night rats and various pests harassed the defenseless men. By day, screams of terror prevailed as various inmates were beaten by interrogators while some were dragged away to be executed.

Outside the prison walls, Judson's beloved wife Ann was frantically trying to procure his release, or, at the very least, obtain permission to visit him and bring him food and comfort. When at last she was allowed to see her husband, she was sorrowed by how quickly his health and appearance had deteriorated. The pair whispered together and Ann was able to inform Adoniram that, fearing their home would be ransacked by unsympathetic neighbors, she had hidden some money and his most precious possession—the Bible manuscripts he had been translating into Burmese—in a deep hole in the yard. Adoniram conveyed his fear that the fruit of his labor and passion would succumb to the elements. He urged his wife to find a way to sneak them into the jail where he could personally safeguard them.

Ann Judson was an intelligent, brave, and creative woman. She returned to the house, dug up the collection of testaments, and carefully concealed them in a soiled old bed pillow. She stitched the seams securely and on her next visit with Adoniram, presented it to him along with some food.

Judson had been at a point of despair. He found himself wishing—praying even—that the Lord would deliver him by hastening his death. But Ann's loving gesture encouraged him and he found his sufferings easier to endure. He must live on and finish his work.

ADONIRAM JUDSON WAS born in Malden, Massachusetts in 1788 to devout parents. His father was pastor of a Congregational church. The Judsons had hopes their brilliant young son would follow in his father's footsteps. But Adoniram's personal habits and lifestyle were a bit on the wild side and at university he was befriended by Professor Jacob Eames, a staunch and persuasive skeptic. Under Eames's influence, Judson's resentment toward Christianity became deep-seated. Upon graduation the young scholar declared that he would go to New York and make his living as a playwright.

No fame or fortune was to be had in his chosen profession, but Adoniram was too proud to go home in defeat. Restless and seeking direction, he decided to go wandering. One night, weary from his travels, Judson sought shelter for the night at an inn. The innkeeper was sympathetic but said that there was no room available. "Perhaps," he offered, "you might share a room with a poor soul who is gravely ill. He must be attended through the night, you see. But this is all I have."

A. J. took the man up on his offer and entered a small room that was partitioned by a blanket suspended from the ceiling. Throughout the night, Judson was kept awake by his roommate moaning, desperately crying out from fever, and cursing God bitterly. Clearly the man was not long for this world. Adoniram was moved by the poor soul's suffering and unnerved by thoughts of what would become of him after his death. Sometime during the early morning hours, the anguished sounds ceased, and Judson understood the end had come.

Coming downstairs in the morning, A. J. confirmed with the innkeeper that his roommate had passed away. "Who was that poor man?" Judson inquired. "A university professor by the name of Eames," the proprietor replied. This sent a chill through the rebellious traveler as he recalled the many discussions he had had with his atheist friend. Immediately he pondered what sort of eternity awaited him. He mounted his horse and galloped home to address his fears among his God-fearing family and friends.

Full of spiritual questions and hungry for answers, Adoniram Judson enrolled in Andover Theological Seminary and by 1809 fully surrendered his life to the Lord Jesus Christ. It was full speed ahead for the young, zealous Christian. Soon he felt the call of God to become a missionary. He read everything he could about missionaries, especially William Carey. Prayer and research led him to focus on the nation of Burma. He learned about Buddhist beliefs and culture. He studied Hebrew and Greek and dreamed of presenting the Burmese people with their own Scriptures. But alas, there were no mission societies in America to send him. Ridiculed by family and fellow students for what they felt was surely a misguided ambition, Judson continued to pursue his call. He and a few like-minded seminary students began meeting for prayer secretly behind stacks of hay. God responded to their intercession and in 1810, when the lads presented a proposal to the association of Congregational ministers, the assembly granted their request, and the first ever American missions board was formed—The American Board of Commissioners for Foreign Missions.

Everything came together for the first American missionary in February 1812. All in the same month Adoniram Judson married Ann Hasseltine, received his ordination, and set sail for Calcutta, India with his brand new bride.

Because of the limited space allotted to the telling of the

Judsons' fascinating story, I will highlight some of the countless struggles and sufferings that awaited them as they began their heavenly endeavor. The sea voyage was lengthy and treacherous. The ship leaked and put them in peril while hasty repairs were conducted. Ann became weakened and ill with severe seasickness. And when they landed in India, intending to meet with William Carey and his co-workers, the reality of the political difficulties of the region hit them full force. The East India Company refused to grant them the necessary permission to remain, ordering them to go to England. They managed to evade the authorities for quite a while until suitable passage could be arranged. By God's providence, the Judsons secured a place on the Portuguese vessel *Georgiana*, which just so happened to be making a stop at Rangoon, Burma before continuing the journey. Ann was pregnant with their first child, and sadly during the monsoon-ravaged sea voyage across the Bay of Bengal, the baby was stillborn.

Heart-broken, Adoniram and Ann disembarked at Rangoon. The Judsons had heard stories of huge pagodas covered in gold. Instead, they found Rangoon to be a filthy, overgrown village, with naked children, wild dogs, and pigs roaming garbage-filled streets. They found refuge in the home of William Carey's son Felix and his Burmese wife. The Careys had planned to leave Rangoon in two weeks' time and had been praying about who would watch over their home. They set the Judsons up with a housekeeper, cook, and language tutor and went on their way. Both Adoniram and Ann plunged into learning the Burmese language immediately—studying for as many as twelve hours a day. A. J. was ready to begin the work that God had called him to do.

The early years at Rangoon were fraught with hardships, sorrows, and no spiritual fruit. Tropical diseases wracked their bodies. Ann bore another child, but he died in infancy. Adoniram preached and shared the gospel daily in the marketplaces, but no one would listen. He and Ann wrote and printed Burmese gospel tracts and prayed about what to do. Then it came to him. It was customary for travelers and others to sit and chat in long open buildings called *zayats*. Adoniram built one of his own and discovered that men were more than willing to rest in the shade and discuss various topics—including the religion founded by a man named Jesus.

The first few converts energized the Judsons. A church was established in Rangoon. It grew. Ann began a school for women and children. Young men were discipled and sent out to evangelize. Adoniram continued his translation work, completing the Gospel of Matthew and beginning the Book of Acts.

But then the political tides turned in Burma. A new king came to power, a cruel king who executed his subjects on a whim and was not at all favorable to the intrusion of "strange" religions in his domain. Adoniram Judson was bold enough (or foolish enough) to travel to the capital city of Ava and plead with the king for leniency. Through a series of events, Ann and Adoniram decided to relocate to Ava where they hoped to evoke a change in government policy. They reluctantly left their work in Rangoon in the hands of others.

Things went from bad to worse when the British declared war on Burma in 1824. Here is where we began the Judsons' story. Adoniram was abducted from his home as a British spy and suffered cruel torments in the government prison. Ann rescued the Bible manuscripts her husband was distressed about and brought them to him concealed within a hard, heavy pillow. The cruel jailer confiscated even that small comfort from the missionary leaving A. J. distraught once again. But Ann was more cunning than her enemies. She hurried home and designed a soft, comfortable, brand new pillow which Adoniram was able to trade with the jailer for his old "worthless" pillow.

One day, quite unexpectedly, the prisoners were rousted from sleep and prepared to move. All their personal belongings were thrown into a heap in the yard. The inmates were chained together and forced along a ten-mile route in the burning sun. Their bare feet became horribly blistered and more than a few of them did not survive the trek. Ann sleuthed out where they had gone and followed after by boat and by oxcart. She was weak with sickness herself at this time but continued to petition for her husband's release at every opportunity.

By God's mercy, Adoniram was finally set free. When the Judsons reunited there was cause for both sorrow and rejoicing. Both Ann and the third child born to her, a daughter, were emaciated, ill, and in need of recuperation. But remarkably, it was discovered that the pillow with the precious treasure concealed within had been plucked

"If I had not felt certain that every additional trial was ordered by infinite love and mercy, I could not have survived my accumulated suffering."
—Adoniram Judson

from the trash heap by one of the Burmese converts who desired it as a memento of his beloved pastor. God, once again, showed Himself mighty in protecting His Word.

In the end the legacy left behind by the Judsons was huge. The Burmese Bible Adoniram translated was a fruitful and lasting work which is still in use to this day. Ann was the first missionary to learn Siamese and had begun to translate the Bible into that language, completing the Gospel of Matthew. The first American missionaries to serve on foreign soil, they left behind more than seven thousand converts as well as thriving churches and schools. But the price they paid to live as guardians of the Word was high. Ann died young, having lost all of her children as a result of harsh conditions and tropical diseases. Adoniram went on to marry again—to a godly woman who served him well but preceded him in death. The Burmese missionary was advised to take a sea voyage to recuperate from a lingering illness. He died on that voyage in 1850 and was buried at sea.

> Later in the 19th century, one of Adoniram's only surviving sons, Edward, speaking at the dedication of the Judson Memorial Church in New York City, summarized his father's story:
>
> Suffering and success go together. If you are succeeding without suffering, it is because others before you have suffered; if you are suffering without succeeding, it is that others after you may succeed.[110]

Robert and Mary Moffat (1795-1883) to South Africa

NIGHTS WERE LONG in Scotland in the winter months. Mother Moffat filled the evening hours by reading exciting missionary tales to young Robert and his six brothers and sisters. It was no secret to any of the Moffat children that their parents prayed not only for the salvation of their souls, but also that the Lord would give some of them the call to serve in a faraway someday.

At around age twenty, while working as an apprentice gardener in England, Robert came upon a handbill announcing a missionary convention of sorts. Intrigued, he attended the gathering and felt the call of God to change the course of his entire life. He applied to the London Missionary Society and was accepted for service to Africa. Around this same time, the young man became enamored with Mary Smith, the daughter of his employer. Mary's desires were right in step with Robert's, for she too longed to work for the Lord among unbelievers in spiritually dark places.

Her parents, however, would not consent to the couple's plans to wed if it meant losing their daughter to a distant land. Robert and Mary never considered forsaking the purposes of God. They parted, trusting God that He would reunite them in His time. In 1816 Robert Moffat set sail for Cape Town, South Africa.

After a few months in Cape Town, Moffat headed for his assignment—a place called Namaqualand about three hundred miles north. Along the way, he met a curious Dutch farmer who wanted to know if the Scotsman was aware of what sort of land he was headed to.

"Not the garden of Eden, of course," said Robert, stating the obvious.

The farmer responded:

> A garden of misery, you mean! You'll find nothing but sand and stones, few people, and each suffering from awful thirst; plains and hills roasted like a burnt leaf under the scorching rays of a cloudless sky! And the chief of the country, Africaner, will set you up as a mark for his boys to shoot at; or mayhap make a drinking cup of your skull, or make a drum of your skin, to dance to.[111]

Moffat, however, was undaunted. Further, the missionary learned this notorious chief had a bounty on his head; the authorities were offering a $1,000 reward for his capture or, for his murder. Afrikaner was a wanted man because of attacks and repeated threats against the Boer farmers who had enslaved his people.

Young Robert found the land itself to be as inhospitable as the Dutch farmer had described. In addition, the vicinity was plagued by snakes, lions, and noisome insects of various kinds. The residents of that land were known as the Hottentots. (The term Hottentot came from Dutch settlers and roughly translates "stutters". The label was applied because of the clicking sound in-

ROBERT MOFFAT

corporated in the language of the non-Bantu tribesmen of the region. A more appropriate name for this people group is Khoekhoe.) And when the missionary encountered their fierce chief, Jager Afrikaner, he was relieved to discover the man was not at all what he had feared. Afrikaner had come to realize that he was actually "the chief of sinners" after hearing the gospel through the testimony of a Christian who had passed through the land. Moffat found the chief to be a changed man who was eager to learn from him and grow in his Christian faith.

In 1819 Mary Smith arrived to join her fiancé. Robert brought Afrikaner with him when he went to Cape Town to collect his bride. The purpose for having the chief accompany him was to prove to the authorities he was no longer a threat to anyone and the price on his head could be rescinded. This objective was achieved after the governor of Cape Town quizzed Jager on his knowledge of the Bible and concluded that he had turned from his violent ways.

After the Moffats were wed, it was decided they should settle in Kuruman and begin a work there. They found the people there severely hostile to missionaries. The village's rainmaker put the blame for the severe drought upon the newcomers. Robert's long black beard frightened away the clouds, it was decided. A group of spear-wielding men surrounded the couple and demanded they leave at once. Robert was fearless. He made it known they had come to serve the Bechuana (as the residents were then known. Now known as the Tswana) and nothing would compel them to leave before they had even begun their work. "Besides," he added, "death is the pathway to our home in heaven." The chief was impressed with the missionary's courage and ordered the spearmen to disperse.

The work among the Bechuana was slow and difficult. Robert toiled to master the local dialect, develop a written language, and begin to translate the Scriptures. He received no help from the natives, for they purposely taught him the wrong words and then ridiculed him for his absurd expressions.

Throughout the years of patient sowing Robert and Mary never doubted that the day of reaping would come. A friend in England wrote to Mary and asked her if there was anything helpful that she might send to them. By faith, Mrs. Moffat responded that they could use a communion set, though as yet there was not even one convert in their midst. By the time the requested gift arrived, the harvest had come. The chalice and plate set was a cherished element at their very first church service and a tangible reminder of the Lord's faithfulness. Mary Moffat wrote:

> We were as those that dreamed. The hour had arrived on which the whole energies of our souls has been fixed, when we should see a church, however small, gathered from among a people who had so long boasted that neither Jesus nor we, His servants, should ever see Bechuanas worship and confess Him as their King.[112]

The Moffats rejoiced as men and women experienced repentance of their grievous sins. There was evidence throughout the tribe that lives had been truly changed by the regenerating work of the Holy Spirit. Prayer meetings were being held and a thriving church was active in evangelizing neighboring tribes.

During the twenty-three years of living and working in Africa, a large and fruitful mission station was established in Kuruman. The Moffats felt it was time for a visit home to England. The entire New Testament had been translated into Bechuana, and the purpose of the trip was to have it printed up so it could be distributed by African Christians. The trip also resulted in another fortunate divine appointment. Robert Moffat met a young man named David Livingston and was able to persuade him to come to Africa to help spread the work. Moffat told Livingston, "I have seen in the morning sun the smoke of a thousand villages where no missionary has ever been!"[113]

The Moffats had not yet finished their work in Africa, so they returned. When the Lord Himself at last declared their work was done, the legacy they left behind was huge. David Livingstone had married the Moffat's oldest daughter and embarked on his historic trail-blazing trek across all of Africa. In fact, five of the Moffat children had devoted their lives to mission work in Africa. The Bechuana (Tswana) translation of the entire Bible had been completed. The life-giving, life-changing Word of God was in the hands of the people who so desperately needed it. And this was a work which remained long after Robert and Mary had gone to their heavenly reward.

Samuel Ajayi Crowther (1809–1891) to Nigeria

NOT ALL BIBLE translators are white Europeans or Americans. Twelve-year-old Ajayi was captured by Muslim slave raiders from his home in Nigeria. Also taken were his family and his whole village. The captors sold the entire lot to Portuguese slave traders who loaded them onto a loathsome ship for transport to the Americas. There the human commodities would be split up and sold to the highest bidder. The British Royal Navy was patrolling the seas with the intention of disrupting all slave trade which had been banned in the British Empire since the early 1800s. The Portuguese ship was intercepted. Ajayi and the other Nigerian captives were liberated and taken to Freetown in Sierra Leone.

Ajayi was cared for by the Anglican Church Missionary Society (CMS) which provided the young lad with an education. He excelled in his studies and quickly acquired the English language. His learning also encompassed Christian education which he also embraced with enthusiasm. In 1825 Ajayi became a full convert, got baptized, and changed his name to Samuel Crowther after one of the founders of the CMS. Samuel explains:

> [A]bout the third year of my liberation from the slavery of man, I was convinced of another worse state of slavery, namely, that of sin and Satan. It pleased the Lord to open my heart . . . I was admitted into the visible Church of Christ here on earth as a soldier to fight manfully under his banner against our spiritual enemies.[114]

The missionaries in Freetown recognized young Samuel's aptitude for learning languages and arranged for him to go to England for further education. There Crowther studied Latin and Greek. While still at the university he began to compile lexicons of different African dialects.

In 1843 Samuel Crowther received his ordination in the Anglican Church. He was sent to the region of Ogun in the nation of his birth, Nigeria. Here he began translating the Scriptures into the Yoruba language, a project which was not completed until 1880. Along the way, Crowther translated portions of the Bible into the Igbo and Nupe languages.

The former slave was skilled in evangelism and apologetics. He penned a series of tracts geared toward revealing to Muslims and animists the errors of their beliefs and enlightening them to the truth of the gospel of Jesus Christ.

Some twenty years later, Reverend Crowther was consecrated as Bishop of the Niger and charged with the task of evangelizing and establishing churches in the most remote regions of Nigeria. He wasted no time in making his mark and the mark of the Lord in that vast land. Mission stations were established, schools opened, churches planted, leadership appointed. If any missionary he sent or any pastor he installed had skill in translation work, Samuel passionately urged his brothers to get the Word of God into the common language of the people they served.

Sadly, the end of Samuel Crowther's ministry was accompanied by disappointment and controversy. His tenure as bishop came at a critical time in the history of British Imperialism in Africa. The "Niger Mission" was an experiment implemented by the forward-thinking Henry Venn. Venn promoted the philosophy that foreign missions should be self-sustaining and thus, indigenous leadership should be installed and empowered wherever possible. After Henry Venn's death, the Anglican Church sent a committee to Nigeria to evaluate the success or failure of the "Niger Mission." The committee's report was scathing. They found fault with the leadership Crowther had selected; the demeanor of the students in the schools; and the interaction between the mission stations, the government, and the business community. In writing about this episode, some analysts attribute the negative report to racism. African newspapers reporting on these events certainly saw it that way.

> "The importance of the future of that mission in connection with the race question cannot be overstated. Men are now asking everywhere whether it is really the intention of the Committee of the CMS, viewing all that has happened and is happening, in the course of the present year, to eliminate completely all native and (black) foreign element from the agency and direction

of a mission which has been under the guidance of Bishop Crowther and his fellow native assistants during a period of over thirty years." —Sierra Leone Weekly News, 11. October 1890, p. 5.[115]

A contributing factor could be the rise of the Theory of Evolution in British circles which had persuaded some to believe the Negro was lower on the evolutionary scale and incapable of leading with authority. Others attached the rising Nigerian call for independence as a threat to the British hold over the region. Whatever the underlying motivations, the Anglican evaluation committee's visit resulted in a mass removal of African clergy, and the vacancies were filled with white British clerics only.

Sadly, the stress of this disappointment took a toll on Crowther. He suffered a stroke and died in 1891. But regardless of how the politics of religion played itself out in this situation, the fruit of Samuel Crowther's work and ministry are evident. Christianity is still alive and well throughout Nigeria, and Bibles are available in many of the dialects of the land.

My tongue shall speak of Your Word,
For all Your commandments are righteous.
Psalm 119:172

HUDSON TAYLOR

10

Hudson Taylor

Strength in Weakness

L ike William Carey, much has been written about the great missions innovator, Hudson Taylor (1832-1905). For example, *Hudson Taylor's Spiritual Secret* by Dr. and Mrs. Howard Taylor, has been a Christian classic since it was first published in 1932. Hudson Taylor served in China during one of the most tumultuous times in Chinese history. He survived the Taiping Rebellion and witnessed violent riots and ethnic massacres right outside his dwelling. Taylor was a bold soul. His passion was to go where no missionary had ever gone before, and it seemed that nothing would stop him—not war, nor lack of funds, nor disease. Yet it was at a point in his life when he was struck down by a debilitating disease that God's greatest work of all was accomplished through him.

From earliest childhood in Yorkshire, England, Hudson Taylor was convinced he had been called by God to be a missionary to China. After a brief period of spiritual rebellion in his teen years, young Hudson began pursuing his goal with renewed vigor. He embarked in radical preparation all on his own. He diligently studied the Mandarin language, painstakingly copying and memorizing the pictograph lettering far into the night hours. To ready his body for the rigors of mission life, he purposely lived in poverty, including limiting himself to a near starvation diet and replacing his bed with a thin mat which he placed on the floor.

I have become all things to all men, that I might by all means save some.

1 Corinthians 9:22

Hudson Taylor apprenticed himself to a local physician. This enabled him to acquire medical knowledge and surgical skills which would open many doors for him to share the gospel of Christ both in the poorest communities in London and eventually in China. In this strict disciplined way of living, Hudson Taylor learned to rely upon his Lord for every need—big or small. This became the hallmark of his future ministry.

Commissioned as a medical missionary, Taylor landed in Shanghai, China, in 1854. His hopes and high expectations were immediately dashed. The funds which were supposed to be waiting for him had not arrived, and there was no word from his mission board as to when he might expect them. No one was anticipating his arrival. No lodging had been arranged. It was providential that Hudson had learned to rely upon God alone.

And though it cannot be stated that the pathway was smooth, God proved Himself faithful as always. A bed was provided for him by a missionary couple; this would suffice for a time.

As he began to get his bearings in the crowded, violent, noisy city of Shanghai, Taylor was frustrated to learn that all the foreigners—including the missionaries—were forbidden to travel beyond a few of the coastal cities. The missionaries sequestered themselves together within a compound and—as it seemed to the perceptive, zealous newcomer—did nothing much but socialize with one another. This would not do for the ambitious man, and almost at once he began to set himself apart from the "ordinary" mission worker.

Hudson Taylor took to the streets, preaching in Mandarin on the street corners and in the marketplaces. He quickly perceived that his appearance was strange to Chinese eyes and this frightened the people. He needed to somehow blend in. He dyed his blonde curly hair black and pulled it back tightly to his scalp. To this he affixed a black braided queue (pigtail). He adopted the awkward, uncomfortable Chinese dress. This consisted of a loose-fitting shirt with overly long sleeves which covered the hands, an embroidered tunic which hung down over baggy pants, and funny shoes with curled up toes. These changes in appearance were met with ridicule and disdain from fellow missionaries. To the Chinese he still looked a bit strange, but they were no longer frightened of him and sometimes stopped to listen as he preached. They also began coming to him for medical treatment.

Taylor sought out opportunities to make evangelistic excursions inland—dozens of them. He (and any fellow-missionary he could persuade to accompany him in this illegal, clandestine endeavor) sailed up the Huangpu River distributing Mandarin Bibles and tracts.

Young Taylor settled in the city of Ningpo for a period of

time. Here he partnered with Dr. William Parker to set up a hospital and medical clinic. This proved to be a busy ministry with Parker and Taylor treating up to two hundred patients a day. Despite the hectic schedule, his Christian mandate was not neglected. Street preaching continued, converts were won to Christ, and a small church began to take root and grow.

After six arduous years in China, the fatigue of tireless work, the spiritual burden for the lost, poor diet, and difficult living conditions, overtook the medical missionary. Hudson Taylor was stricken with a debilitating illness. The diagnosis was hepatitis, but certainly exhaustion and possibly depression also played a part. The prognosis was grim. Unless he received full and complete rest, he would not recover from this illness. In 1860 Taylor reluctantly agreed to return to London to salvage his health.

Though most of his colleagues feared he would never return to his beloved China, this was not the conviction held by Hudson Taylor. "Millions a month" of Chinese men and women were perishing without the knowledge of the Savior. No, he was not done with China. He would never be done until God called him home.

So, as he convalesced in London, Taylor prayed. In Ningpo he had begun translating the New Testament into the regional dialect. Unfortunately, duties at the hospital and at the fledgling church had not afforded him the time to dedicate himself to this task. Here on his sickbed with books and manuscripts scattered about, the translation work flourished. He was able to devote nine to twelve hours a day to this important project. The Ningpo New Testament was sent to the printer in short order.

Taylor prayed. He prayed for the lost in China. He prayed for workers for the harvest. He prayed for the Western church to awaken from complacency and be moved to action. And as he prayed and sought the Lord in His holy Word, the answer came. A new kind of missions agency was needed. A new kind of missionary was required. Hudson wrote in his diary:

> In the study of that Divine Word I learned that, to ob-
> tain successful labourers, not elaborate appeals for help
> were needed; but, first, earnest prayer to God to thrust
> forth labourers; and, second, the deepening of the spiri-
> tual life of the Churches, so that men should be unable
> to stay at home. I saw that the Apostolic plan was, not to
> raise ways and means, but *to go and do the work*, trusting
> in His sure word who has said: "Seek ye first the king-
> dom of God, and His righteousness; and all these things
> shall be added unto you."[116]

An extended time in confinement to a sickbed, far removed
from the field of his calling, would seem to some to be the least
productive period in Taylor's life. On the contrary, during this
lowest point the greatest fruit was born. The China Inland
Mission (CIM) was conceived that day. This would be a mission
of prayer and of faith. The major characteristic that set CIM apart
from other agencies and societies that had come before was neither the mission itself nor the missionaries who were sent would
engage in fundraising of any sort. God Himself would supply all
material and financial needs in response to faithful prayer.

For the first time ever, single women could also be sent out
to the field. The missionaries commissioned by CIM would be
men and women of prayer, unconcerned with their own comfort. Other missionaries of the time desired to not only hold to
their British ways, but to transplant them onto foreign soil as
well. CIM missionaries must be willing to identify with the host
culture in their dress and diets. "In all things not sinful, let us
become like the Chinese that we may save some," Taylor told
them—a reflection of the apostle Paul's words in 1 Corinthians
9:19-22.

> For though I am free from all men, I have made myself a
> servant to all, that I might win the more; and to the Jews
> I became as a Jew, that I might win Jews; to those who
> are under the law, as under the law, that I might win
> those [who are] under the law; to those who are without
> law, as without law (not being without law toward God,
> but under law toward Christ), that I might win those
> who are without law; to the weak I became as weak, that
> I might win the weak. I have become all things to all
> men, that I might by all means save some.

Taylor was excited about this new mandate from God. He immediately began to put it into practice. He prayed for twenty-four new missionaries. God answered.

And that was just the beginning. In 1881, he asked God for seventy missionaries; he got seventy-six. In 1886, he prayed for an additional one hundred workers; one hundred two candidates responded. And so it continued.

Those missionaries went out to every province in China. They evangelized, planted churches, translated Scripture, and built schools and hospitals. They trained up Chinese Christians who also learned to pray and walk by faith.

In 1900, the tragedy called The Boxer Rebellion occurred. Foreigners and their ideas were deemed a threat. Hundreds of missionaries were executed along with Chinese Christians. CIM lost fifty-eight missionaries and twenty-one missionary children. This was, understandably, devastating to Hudson Taylor who felt a fatherly responsibility for those who had answered his call to service. But as so often happens, persecution stirred up the church to bold response; 933 brave Christian soldiers responded to the call to serve in China.

The work that began in the prayer closet of one faithful man resulted in the gospel seed being sown throughout the vast remote areas of China where the name of Christ had never been heard. Today, it is reported that there may be as many as thirty-one million Christians in China. And the ministry of China Inland Mission also endures, taking the gospel beyond the shores of China under the name of OMF— Overseas Missionary Fellowship.

Fruit Born Out of Weakness

WE ALL LOVE the inspiring stories of the mighty ones. Heroes in the eyes of all, these brave saints have conquered enemies, and overcome difficulties, trials and temptations. They have preached powerful sermons and had throngs respond to the gospel. They have refuted dignitaries in courtrooms and palaces. They have stood and prayed in fiery furnaces and survived a dark night among hungry lions.

Hudson Taylor's story stands in contrast to these. His testimony resonates with the "weak" saints—the feeble, the aged, the silent, the bedridden. There are many believers whose prayers for healing or deliverance are not answered in the straight-forward way they might hope. Small, weak, insignificant in the eyes of the world, and sadly, sometimes even to the church—how could these Christians be of any use at all in the kingdom of God? Perhaps this describes your own present reality, and you are feeling your days of useful service to God are over.

Take heart! Thankfully, God's ways are much higher than our ways. He very frequently uses the weak things of the world to display His mighty power. It is true that "we have this treasure in earthen vessels [jars of clay] that the excellency of the power may be of God and not of us" (2 Corinthians 4:7).

For example, Paul the Apostle was in the midst of a fruitful ministry. He had brought the gospel of salvation through Christ to the Gentile world. He planted churches, trained pastors, worked mighty miracles. He wrote most of the New Testament! Then he was waylaid or hindered by an unspecified thorn in the flesh. Many believe this was some sort of physical malady. Paul prayed for it to be removed. He repeated his request three times. Then God answered in an unexpected way. Paul testified it was at this low point, a point of helplessness and need, that he was able to experience the power of God resting upon him.

> And lest I should be exalted above measure by the abundance of the revelations, a thorn in the flesh was given to me, a messenger of Satan to buffet me, lest I be exalted above measure. Concerning this thing I pleaded with the Lord three times that it might depart from me. And He said to me, "My grace is sufficient for you, for My strength is made perfect in weakness." Therefore most gladly I will rather boast in my infirmities, that the power of Christ may rest upon me. Therefore I take pleasure in infirmities, in reproaches, in needs, in persecutions, in distresses, for Christ's sake. For when I am weak, then I am strong. (2 Corinthians 12:7-10)

The Book of Genesis tells us that Joseph was sold into slavery by his own brothers. But it got even worse! He was thrown into prison (a dungeon) because of the false accusation of his master's wife. However, while there, Joseph used his gift of dream interpretation; which led to him being called upon to interpret Pharaoh's dream; which happened to be about the coming famine. The Pharaoh entrusted Joseph with the task of storing up food in preparation for the future shortage. This not only provided food for the entire kingdom but also saved Joseph's own family from starvation. Such a mighty deliverance at the hands of a prisoner/slave!

God passed over the strong, strapping young men among Jesse's sons in picking Israel's leader. The Lord told the prophet

Samuel, "Do not look at his appearance or at his physical stature, because I have refused him. For *the LORD does* not *see* as man sees; for man looks at the outward appearance, but the LORD looks at the heart" (1 Samuel 16:7). Instead, God chose David, a small, insignificant shepherd boy to bring down a giant and deliver Israel's army.

Mercifully, God does not see people the way we often do. Neither does God see us the way we frequently see ourselves. If you feel you are looking at your days of usefulness in the rearview mirror . . . If you are currently physically, emotionally, or intellectually challenged in some way . . . If you are hindered or limited by circumstances beyond your control—Don't give up! God sees. He knows. He is still able to let His power and His glory shine through you. And He desires to do so.

In Holland during World War II, the Ten Boom family heroically sheltered Jews to save them from the Holocaust. Then they were betrayed, and the Nazis took them away where they faced the same horrors as their Jewish friends. Sisters Corrie and Betsie struggled to continue sharing the love of Christ even in the depths of hell. Betsie was convinced the Lord would get them out somehow and "when He does," she told Corrie, "we must tell everyone the truth we have discovered here—that there is no pit so deep the love of God is not deeper still."

Betsie ten Boom perished in that horrible camp. Corrie was released through a clerical error. She followed through on the agreement with her beloved sister. She traveled ceaselessly as "a tramp for the Lord" speaking in sixty-four countries over the course of thirty-three years. Yes, she told the heart-wrenching story as depicted in the book and the movie of her life, *The Hiding Place*. But she also told a story of forgiveness and the deep, deep love of God that permeated the rest of her years.

At age eighty-four Corrie ten Boom felt God direct her to

begin praying for a new ministry. Little did she know the sort of difficult ministry God had in store for her. A few years later, a series of strokes left her weak, feeble, and unable to speak. Mostly confined to bed in her small room, Corrie painstakingly communicated to her companions with a collection of nods and blinks. Yet even then, she clearly reflected the love of Christ to those who came to visit her. And she ventured far beyond the walls of her bedroom as she prayed. Corrie interceded for those who wrote to her, and for those countless thousands that had been touched by her decades-long speaking ministry. She was fruitful, useful to the kingdom of God to the end.

Remember the word to Your servant,
Upon which You have caused me to hope.
This is my comfort in my affliction,
For Your word has given me life.
Psalm 119:49-50

Life is but a Weaving (the Tapestry Poem)

by Grant Colfact Tullar

Often recited by Corrie ten Boom

My life is but a weaving
Between my God and me.
I cannot choose the colors
He weaveth steadily.

Oft' times He weaveth sorrow;
And I in foolish pride
Forget He sees the upper
And I the underside.

Not 'til the loom is silent
And the shuttles cease to fly
Will God unroll the canvas
And reveal the reason why.

The dark threads are as needful
In the weaver's skillful hand
As the threads of gold and silver
In the pattern He has planned

He knows, He loves, He cares;
Nothing this truth can dim.
He gives the very best to those
Who leave the choice to Him.[117]

CAMERON TOWNSEND

11

Cameron Townsend

and Wycliffe Bible Translators

Young Californian William Cameron Townsend (1896-1982) was just twenty-one years old when he embarked on his first mission assignment in Guatemala along with his friend Elbert "Robby" Robinson. In Guatemala City the pair was welcomed by the staff of Central American Mission. After Cam and Robby had been shown to their room and began unpacking, the team evaluated the new recruits. "Robinson will do fine," one said. "But that skinny Townsend won't last two months."

Townsend and Robinson had been sent out as Bible salesmen representing The Bible House in Los Angeles. After a brief orientation, Edward Bishop, the area director for Central American Mission, told the boys, "As Scripture salesmen, you boys will sow the seed where there are no evangelical congregations. It won't be easy. But you'll have our prayers and God will help you." Cameron Townsend had prayed his ministry would be modeled after the life of Hudson Taylor and so this was just the type of challenge that Cam was hoping for. Bishop was anxious to get them out among the people. He invited them to accompany him to a Bible conference he would be holding in the mountain city of Antigua. "You can start selling your Bibles there," Bishop informed them.

At the conference the novice missionaries heard heroic stories from the locals about the dangers of evangelizing among the Catholic strongholds of the rural communities. When the conference was dismissed the following day, the attendees were sent out to preach the gospel as they headed home.

Young Cam was filled with nervousness. He had never even attempted such street witnessing at home in English, let alone here in this foreign land—and in Spanish yet!

When the meeting ended, he excused himself and hurried up a street alone. He didn't want anyone, not even Robby, to watch. Turning the corner, he approached a man standing near the curb. Opening his mouth to speak, he found he could make no sound; he walked on past with a pounding heart. Twice more he tried but could not summon the courage to speak. A block further on he came upon a young man more his age. "Lord, help me," he prayed fervently.

Having read a good opening question was, "Do you know the Lord Jesus?" Cam asked in halting Spanish, "¿Conoces al Señor Jesús?" The Guatemalan's dark face showed puzzlement. "No, I'm a stranger in town myself," he replied in Spanish. "I don't know the fellow."

Cam hadn't realized in Spanish señor may mean *Lord* or *mis-*

ter and that Jesús is a common name in Latin American countries.

> Feeling a total failure, Cam fled down the cobblestone
> street to his room. Dropping on his knees and burying
> his face in the bed, he cried, "Lord, I'm a failure."[118]

Following this disheartening fiasco, the humbled Townsend
learned he was assigned to sell Bibles and Christian literature
in the towns inhabited by the Cakchiquel Indians. He had no
choice but to apply the lessons learned and persevere with the
Lord's help.

Pastor Isidro Alarcon, the Guatemalan pastor of the
Christian congregation in Antigua, became his guide. As they
hiked along the dusty trails, Pastor Isidro regaled Cam (whom the
Guatemalans had dubbed don Guillermo—Spanish for William)
about the story of how the gospel had first come to this territory.

A man named Silverio Lopez, who was one of the few
Cakchiquels who could read and write, purchased a Spanish Bible
on a visit to Guatemala City. He found it difficult to understand
and put it aside. When he returned to his village, he learned his
young daughter was very ill. As was the custom, he entreated the
witchdoctor who told Lopez to purchase candles from the church
and burn them before the icons to dispel the evil spirits. The cost
of the candles along with the witchdoctor's fee would put the
poor man heavily in debt.

Walking along the road, contemplating how he would pay
his fee, Lopez found a scrap of paper with this verse: "My Father's
house should be called a house of prayer, but you have made it a
den of thieves" (Matthew 21:13). At home he found his Bible and
discovered this verse was contained in it. He headed to the near-
est sizeable town and purchased proper medicine for his child.

"Then he looked me up," Isidro Alarcon told Townsend,

"and I told him how to believe. That was only six months ago. He has since led forty Indians to Christ."[119]

The following morning, Townsend was determined to put his earlier evangelism disappointment behind him and began a hut-to-hut campaign. He would knock on the doorpost of a hut, quote John 3:16 in Spanish and offer his literature. He quickly learned a lesson in proper Cakchiquel etiquette after a scraggly guard dog bit him on the ankle: the custom was to call out to the residents from beyond the cornstalk fence and wait to be invited into the yard.

After a few days of doing this, Cam came upon a man sitting in a shady place drinking an alcoholic beverage. The fellow declined the tract that he was handed. "Sorry, señor, but I cannot read." As the Bible salesman turned to walk away, the man stopped him. "My friend can read. Sell me your book and I will have him read it to me." Townsend obliged and invited the man, whose name was Tiburcio, to the believers' meeting on Sunday. Not only did Tiburcio show up on Sunday, but he gave his life to Christ that day causing don Guillermo's morale to soar. This was the very first person he had ever helped to find salvation.

As he continued his campaign in San Antonio and a few surrounding villages, Townsend gained valuable insights into Central American life. He learned the native rural inhabitants were at the very bottom of the social status. They were unbelievably poor, uneducated, and frequently taken advantage of. The men were allowed to obtain alcohol on credit, leaving them with huge debts that they could never repay. They were, however, permitted to work off their debt as farmhands to local ranchers, basically becoming slaves of the wealthy *ladinos*. A *ladino* or *mestizo* was a person of mixed Spanish and indigenous heritage who held a high position in society. This situation of poverty and oppression grieved Townsend. He began to see education and the gospel had the potential to not only change individual lives but also have an impact on society as well.

In a remote village, don Guillermo and a guide were accosted by an angry mob that was opposed to what they perceived to be a threat to their religion which combined Catholicism with the Spiritism of the witchdoctors. The local police had to come to the rescue of the two evangelicals. The lesson learned from this encounter became the new protocol for future outreaches. When entering a new village, Cameron would first go to the authorities and present them with a Bible which he paid for himself out of his meagre wages. Then he would ask permission to sell his literature in their jurisdiction. This became Townsend's policy whether entering a remote tribal village or the capital city of a nation.

Cameron had an idea of building a school for Cakchiquel children. He shared his vision with one of his close Cakchiquel friends who enthusiastically began telling everyone. Determined to follow through on this ambitious plan, Townsend solicited and received donations from the governor, other missionaries, and local merchants. He told them that literate and educated nationals would make them better able to contribute to the society as a whole.

> . . . and so in March 1919, Cameron Townsend opened what is believed to be the first local Indian mission school in Central America, and possibly all of South America. . . .
>
> In inaugurating this milestone in education, Cam was further ahead of his time than anyone realized. Educators in the Americas would long be (and many still are) shackled to the melting pot philosophy of offering schooling to minority linguistic groups in the language of the majority.

> But schooling was not the whole answer. Convinced that the Cakchiquels must have Scripture in their own language, Cam began building a notebook of Cakchiquel expressions. The Indians responded with amazed delight, for he was the first outsider ever to attempt this task.[120]

Townsend found the translation work challenging. The words sounded so similar to his ears that they were difficult to distinguish. He made his Cakchiquel helpers repeat things over and over again. He struggled to make his mouth and vocal cords duplicate the sounds. The grammar seemed to make no sense at all. Verbs had endless prefixes and suffixes applied to indicate time, number, location, and various other attributes. By chance, Cameron ran into an American archaeologist who provided some guidance. "You are trying to force Cakchiquel into the Latin mold," he said. "Try to see it from the Cakchiquel point of view and you'll find the language developed in a logical fashion." This helped to move things along.

Though Townsend felt his grasp of the language was still insufficient for an accurate translation of the Scriptures, he believed even a "temporary" translation of one Gospel would be spiritually beneficial to the Cakchiquel believers. When several chapters of the Gospel of Mark had been completed, he hurried to get them to the printer in the town of Antigua.

The printing press was located in the mayor's office. When the mayor got word of what was to be printed, he objected. "We are trying to eliminate the Indian dialects," he said. "We want everyone to speak Spanish."

> "But you see, your honor," Cam suggested diplomatically, "we have the Indian language on one page and the Spanish on the other. This way they can learn to read

first in their own language and then make an easy shift
into Spanish." . . . The mayor agreed.[121]

Appallingly, don Guillermo's obsession with providing indigenous peoples with the Scriptures in their heart language was also
opposed by other missionaries and by his own mission board.
They felt it was a waste of time and money that could be spent
to evangelize the Spanish-speaking *ladino* population. After all,
these were the movers and shakers of the realm. They controlled
the schools, the government, the businesses — virtually all of
society. In contrast, Cam believed the Cakchiquels and other
minorities would remain second-class citizens who were taken
advantage of by the majority until they could become educated
and self-sufficient enough to stand as equals with the *ladinos*. The
same philosophy applied to evangelism and church growth. If the
Cakchiquel Christians (and others) had the Scriptures in their
own languages, as well as Bible training, the indigenous churches
could grow and thrive and be self-sufficient without being de-
pendent on upper class benefactors. To this end Townsend and
his colleagues created a compound with a school, and medical
clinic. The Bible school taught the Bible. But in addition, the students were given tasks around the compound to help them learn
job skills. Eventually a coffee bean huller was installed which op-
erated as a profit-making business helping to sustain the whole
operation.

Though Cam did not consider himself a scholar, he had lived,
worked, and worshipped alongside the Cakchiquels. He daily ob-
served their conversations, customs, and habits and tenacious-
ly applied what he learned to the study of the language. But
Townsend, following the advice of the archaeologist, pioneered
what came to be known as descriptive linguistics which describes
the grammar of a language from its own point of view. Previously
studies in this field focused on comparing the relationship of one

language to another. The completion of the Cakchiquel grammar in 1926 was a significant contribution to the science of linguistics. When at last the forty-nine-page grammar was printed, Townsend desired to speed up the New Testament translation work.

He grew frustrated when many things—some days it seemed like everything—conspired to distract him from that effort. Eventually he came up with the idea of spending some time away from those distractions. Accompanied by his two best Cakchiquel helpers, Cam retreated to California where the translation work was completed in short order.

In October of 1929, the missionary held an emotional dedication ceremony before the manuscript was sent off to the printer. When the small, bound New Testament returned from the printer, another large celebration and dedication was held in Cakchiquel territory in the village of Patzun. The jubilant Christians shouted repeatedly, "Thanks be to God!" A Cakchiquel pastor concluded the ceremony by declaring, "This Book marks an epoch for us. Each year we should celebrate the twentieth of May as the day upon which we received God's Word in our own language!"

Subsequently, Cameron made an opportunity to present the president of Guatemala with his own personal copy of the Cakchiquel New Testament. In the days and months that followed, this story was relayed to Townsend as a testimony that even a symbolic gift to a high-ranking official could bear fruit for the kingdom of God.

A Cakchiquel Indian was sent by his town to complain to the president about the Protestant workers bothering them about a new religion. The president asked him if he could read. "Yes," he answered, so he was handed a copy of the Cakchiquel New Testament. After reading a few lines, he looked up in amazement. "This is wonder-

ful! God speaks our language! Where can I get a copy
of this book?" "From the people you were complaining
about," the president replied. The spokesman returned
home, bought the book in his own language, and became a believer. Now he goes everywhere telling people
that the president evangelized him.[122]

As much as Cameron Townsend loved his work among the
Cakchiquels, he was still drawn to the tribes who had not been
reached, those who did not have access to a copy of God's Word
that they could understand. He knew there were other tribes in
Guatemala, even more throughout Central America. In South
America there were thousands of Bibleless people scattered
throughout Amazonia. He felt an urgency to mobilize translators
to these vast missionary fields. The few Bible colleges in the States
that offered linguistic training required their students to embark
on a four-year course of learning. This was too long for Cam's
ambitious agenda.

Instead, Townsend conceived of an intensive training course
that zeroed in on key elements allowing a translator to begin
work in a remote tribe in as little as three months. With the help
of like-minded colleagues and financial backers, the "Summer
Institute of Linguistics" was formed. A donated rustic barn in
Sulphur Springs, Arkansas, served as their first campus. Students
would live "rough" so they would be ready for what life was truly
like in the field. Also known as Camp Wycliffe, the first class for
prospective Bible translators was held June to September in 1934.
It consisted of four eager teachers and one student (some sources
say there were two students). Thankfully, the student body increased each year, and as the graduates were sent out, reports of
success began to trickle in from the field.

A particularly fruitful work was realized among the indigenous tribes of Mexico. Through a series of God-orchestrated

interactions with the minister of education and later with the president of Mexico himself, Townsend and his linguists were welcomed with open arms. Their policy of incorporating literacy, education, and economic stability was just what the Mexican government was looking for to unify their diverse population. The president and his ministers also began to recognize the life-changing benefits the Bible was bringing to the nation.

The number of workers on the field increased, and additional new recruits were continually being sought. Then some misunderstandings developed between missionaries on the front lines and folks in the States who were tasked with publicity and fundraising. It was determined the solution was to form two separate organizations with different but complementary functions. The Summer Institute of Linguistics (SIL) would be the banner for overseas workers and their training. This move side-stepped any objections that might be raised by some national authorities who were reluctant to endorse Christian missionaries on their shores.

> The name of the partner organization would be Wycliffe Bible Translators. This non-profit entity would be the face of the work on American soil for fund raising and for publicity. The constitution for WBT adopted the doctrinal statement of the China Inland Mission, long admired by Townsend. It included belief in the divine inspiration of the Bible, the Trinity, the fall of man, the atonement of Christ, justification by faith, the resurrection of the body, eternal life of the saved and eternal punishment of the lost.[123]

Townsend outlined the "distinctive features" of Wycliffe's work as he saw them:

1. We specialize on giving the Scriptures to the tribes without them.

2. We pioneer, going preferably to closed fields.
3. We cooperate with missions, governments, scientific organizations, philanthropic organizations, always cooperate and serve, never compete.
4. We follow the linguistic approach.
5. We dare to follow even when God leads along strange paths.
6. We are not sectarian or ecclesiastical, not even dogmatic. We don't try to force people into any type of denomination or anti-denominational mold.
7. We look to God to raise up the men and the means and to open the doors.
8. We should use all the aids of science, including radio, airplanes, etc., when going to jungle tribes. [Note: This philosophy led to the creation of a third entity, The Jungle Aviation and Radio Service –JAARS.]
9. We expect to finish the task in this generation.[124]

Today this ambitious goal is close to fulfillment in our current generation. The following chapter will reveal the challenges which still lie ahead and also the innovations that are already overcoming them. This has certainly been orchestrated through the wisdom, power, and sovereignty of our mighty Lord. It becomes clear when one engages in any study or discussion on Bible translation for the languages of the world, that thanks must be offered to God for the vision and determination of Cameron Townsend and the decades long work of Wycliffe Bible Translators.

Dayumae (1930-2014) and Rachel Saint (1914-1994)
A Bible for a Tribe of Murderers

DAYUMAE WAS BORN into the Waudani tribe deep in the rain forest of Ecuador. The Waudani (alternate spelling, Huaorani) were primitive people subsisting on the fish they speared in the Curaray River or dining on monkeys which were hunted with poisonous darts. Rather short in stature, both men and women were characterized by shiny straight black hair, elongated pierced earlobes, and clothing that consisted of woven vines tied around their waists. They lived together in a communal hut constructed of palm leaves, sleeping in hammocks suspended from the ceiling.

The tribe was called Auca or "naked savages" by outsiders. The nickname was well deserved, for the tribesmen were quick to attack and spear anyone who offended them—strangers both white and brown, those from neighboring villages, or even someone in their own community who had offended in some way. As well, it was required of the relatives of the murdered one to avenge the killing. This resulted in an endless cycle of murder and revenge. Over one-half of all deaths in the tribe were attributed to violence. It was also the custom of the Waudani to bury living offspring in the grave of a deceased father.

This is where the remarkable story of the young girl Dayumae

DAYUMAE

begins. As her father lay dying after being speared by a foe, he pled with his daughter to flee into the forest to escape being buried alive. She ran, fearing for her life, and realizing she would probably never see her family again. Dayumae felt her chances of survival would be greater among the friendly tribe of the Quechas. She came upon some Quecha girls who lived among the foreigners and followed them home. Home turned out to be a mission compound where Wycliffe Bible translator Rachel Saint was working on putting the Scriptures into tribal languages. Rachel befriended Dayumae and set about learning her language as well.

Then in 1955 one of the most heart-wrenching and inspiring of all missionary stories took place. A few miles away from the hacienda where Rachel Saint was stationed, another group of missionaries, including Rachel's brother, had begun praying and making plans for a way to reach the Waodanis—a task deemed impossible by every missions agency. The five men—Nate Saint, Jim Elliot, Roger Youderian, Ed McCully, and Pete Fleming, as well as their families—felt a dire sense of urgency. The Waodanis, with their violent lifestyle, were actually facing eradication by their own hands. The missionaries were aware that every day these primitive people were deprived of the gospel meant more souls facing eternity without Christ. Knowing the danger of a first encounter with the "savages" Nate and the others began flying over the villages in their little yellow plane, dropping small gifts, and shouting out some phrases they had learned from Dayumae. (More of this part of the story can be found in Elizabeth Elliot's book, *Through Gates of Splendor*.)

The following year the five men set up camp on a sandy beach in Waodani territory. The initial interaction was with a man (Nenkiwi) and two women (one of whom was Gimade, Dayumae's sister). The trio had come to the beachside camp to find out if the white men could tell them what had become of Dayumae, but Nate and the others could not understand what they were asking. The

RACHEL SAINT

missionaries were excited by the friendly encounter which even included taking Nenkiwi for an airplane ride in the "wood bee."

But all was not well. Nate's son Steve fills in the details in his book, *The End of the Spear*. The next day, Nenkiwi was accused of taking improper liberties with Gimade. To turn the ire of the tribe away from himself, Nenkiwi lied and said the foreigners had boasted of killing Dayumae and eating her. The Waodani men grabbed their spears and headed to the beach to exact their revenge. All five of the missionaries were slaughtered and the plane was hacked to pieces.

Recovery operations confirmed the deaths. Any salvageable belongings were retrieved and returned to the grieving families. Among the items was a home movie filmed of the first few days of life around the camp for the five and then of the friendly encounter with Nenkiwi and Gimade. Watching the film in silence with the martyrs' wives and children, Dayumae spotted her sister in the film and cried out. The realization hit her that her friends and loved ones had murdered the loved ones of her new friends and family. The Waodani girl—now a woman —repented in grief and sorrow and gave her heart and life to Christ.

From this point on, she worked diligently alongside Rachel Saint to bring "God's carvings" to life for the Waodani people. Rachel learned that in Wae Tededo (the Waodani language) *Waengongi* was the word for the Creator of all things. She discovered that though the Waodani had great fear of the spirit world, they recognized some preparation was necessary in order to "jump the great boa" into the afterlife. In Waodani theology this entailed proving to *Waengongi* that they were strong because of the number of people they had killed. With the same sense of urgency for lost souls that had driven the five martyrs, Rachel and Dayumae persevered day after day until a Wae Tededo Gospel (and eventually the entire New Testament) became a reality.

Years later some members of Dayumae's tribe found her and urged her to return to her own people. The young Christian woman went with them and astonished everyone in the tribe that she was still alive—that she hadn't been killed and eaten by the foreigners. She boldly told the Waodanis that the men they had killed were good men. Then she said, "Just like you speared the good foreigners, that's how they killed Jesus, God's good son."[125]

The Waodanis wanted to hear more. They told Dayumae to bring the white women to them so they could learn more about what God says in His carvings.

And so it was that Elizabeth Elliot who lost her husband Jim and Rachel Saint who lost her brother Nate at the hands of Waodani, went to live among them. They were the first outsiders to be accepted by the tribe. Instead of seeking revenge, they were able to show God's love and forgiveness.[126]

One by one the Waodanis turned to Jesus their Savior. The things God said in His carvings changed them from "naked savages" to true Christians who desired to reflect the image of God. No longer bloodthirsty, they became evangelists taking the Good News to their former foes in surrounding tribes.

The Elliots and the Saints and the others paid the ultimate price, but their sacrifice was not in vain.

For the word of God is living and powerful,
and sharper than any two-edged sword,
piercing even to the division of soul and
spirit, and of joints and marrow,
and is a discerner of the thoughts
and intents of the heart.
Hebrews 4:12

12

The Impact of Technology and Contemporary Guardians

The preceding chapters of *Guardians of the Word* have emphasized the necessity of making the Bible available to all people in whichever language is most readily understood. That sounds like a very big job. Just how big? Here are some statistics. (Note: the numbers are fluid and vary from source to source. Approximations are used here.)

7,000 = the number of spoken or signed languages in the world today
3,000 = the number of languages which have Scriptures or Scripture portions available
2,200 = the number of Bible translation projects currently underway

1,800 = the number of spoken or signed languages waiting for Bible translation to begin[127]

It certainly *is* a big job. An overwhelming task lies ahead. In the past, the mandate for Bible translators was summarized as: one language, one man (or woman), one lifetime. This takes into account years of learning a target language along with its grammar and idioms; tedious translation work by hand; having the finished manuscript checked and rechecked; then, field tested before sending it abroad for printing and binding. If this mandate (one language, one man, one lifetime) is utilized for the languages which remain Bibleless, in the span of 1,800 plus lifetimes, how many generations of unreached people would perish before having a chance to hear God's own story of a Savior's love? But we know that with God, all things are possible. And, in fact, the impossible is happening today.

Missiologists who keep a close watch on worldwide statistics noticed a dramatic and exciting change at the beginning of the twenty-first century. The gap began to close between the number of Bible projects underway and the number of languages still awaiting the Scriptures. And the pace of Bible translation is accelerating every year. Undoubtedly the grace of God is at work in this. One of the tools in His unlimited arsenal seems to be modern-day technology.

Our Creator God has endowed His human creations with intelligent and resourceful minds. While often man's ingenuity manifests itself for evil devices, God can and does redeem inventions for His purposes. An example of this is Gutenberg's world-changing innovation. As we saw in chapters 3 and 4 of this book, the moveable type press enabled the printed Word of God to be disseminated to the masses. The technology available to Bible translators today makes Gutenberg's advances pale in comparison.

Progress in the travel industry itself has sped up God's work in remote locales. Remember reading about the treacherous months-long sea voyages of Taylor, Carey, and Judson? Today, a missionary can board a jet near his home base and land in any nation he desires within a matter of hours. On the ground, there are various vehicles or other modes of appropriate transport depending on the terrain of the destination.

In the past, field workers would log new vocabulary words on notecards, then write and rewrite their translation efforts in stacks of notebooks. Imagine how taxing on the mind for the translator to try to remember if he or she had come across a particular word or phrase previously. Unless the servant of Christ was gifted with a photographic memory, hours could be spent leafing through pages and files to determine the results of earlier study. And then, sadly, decades' worth of work could be lost through fire, flood, or theft.

Typewriters. Photocopiers. Facsimile machines. These familiar tools seem hardly worth mentioning. It is difficult to remember that though the typewriter came into everyday business usage in 1880; the copier (Xerox) and the fax are relative newcomers (1960 and 1970 respectively). These baby steps in the path of technological advancement were welcomed by those doing important translation projects in foreign fields.

Today, missionaries have access to personal computers, tablets, and smart phones (as we all do). It's astounding to realize there is more computing power in our handheld devices than could be generated by a room-sized bank of computers in the '70s. With email, instant messaging, sophisticated interactive websites, and file transfer capabilities, communication has become instant worldwide. Portable satellite modems make connecting to the internet possible from remote locations virtually anywhere in the world. Never again must a translator fret over the potential destruction of his life's toil. Once the translated manuscript has been uploaded to a remote server, the work is no longer vulnerable to common perils.

Innovative software programs have been developed to streamline various aspects of Bible translation. An example of this is the *Adapt It* software program developed by Wycliffe Associates for the bilingual translator.*[128] When the target text calls for a word that does not carry over from the source language, the translator selects a similar word or phrase to convey the idea required. The next time that same word turns up in subsequent text, the program asks the operator if he or she wants to use the previously inserted word or if a different word would be more appropriate for the new context. Gone are the days of shuffling vocabulary notecards.

Similar software called *Paratext* was developed by the United Bible Societies (UBS). This useful tool can display Hebrew or Greek text in an interlinear fashion alongside the translation in process. Dictionaries and translations in similar languages can also be called up within the software. United Bible Societies also maintains a Digital Bible Library (DBL) to which member translators can upload their finished work. Their goal is to be a global repository for Scripture translations. With many partner and collaborating agencies, the DBL provides a "shared technical infrastructure designed to help accelerate the scripture translation process, provide new insight into the translation development process, and facilitate global access to the Bible."[129] At a glance it is easy to see who is doing what so efforts are not duplicated

---

* Wycliffe Associates (WA) was founded in 1967 as a subgroup within Wycliffe Bible Translators (WBT) (now Wycliffe USA). In 2016 WA split off from WBT and became an entirely separate entity. The detachment occurred when distinct differences in translation protocols and philosophies became irreconcilable.

which would be a waste of valuable resources and prolong the completion of the objective to get the Bible to the entire world.

There are also devices and software which can accommodate audio translation work in dialects that do not yet have a written language. Why waste time developing an alphabet and launching literacy projects when the Word of God can easily be shared with a downloadable audio file?

Other computer programs allow for worldwide translation collaboration through satellite connections. Consultation with a linguistic specialist in Greek, Hebrew, or any other language is only a mouse-click away. Technology can be an amazing thing.

At the beginning of this chapter, we listed 2,200 as the estimated number of translation projects currently underway. There are numerous agencies involved with this endeavor. Just as different churches and denominations have arisen because of nuances in doctrine, practice, and preferences, so it is with Bible translation organizations. There are many different methods and philosophies in play all with the common goal of getting the job done.

Let's take a look at some real-life examples of how modern innovations are being utilized in the task of Bible translation by some of the faithful servants of God working in the world today.

Dima's Story, Tajikistan

When Dima (last name withheld) was a boy growing up in Tajikistan, he was fascinated with video games. As a teen he cajoled his relatives into investing in an entrepreneurial enterprise; he wanted to build a game room in his own neighborhood. Collecting enough money for a secondhand Sony Playstation, Dima converted a portion of the family living room into an arcade and charged his friends by the hour to play against one another. His fascination with electronics continued and by the time he was eighteen, the Tajik boy was teaching himself programming and website building.

Then Dima became a Christian and started using his talents to help Christian ministries develop their online presence. He had an idea to build a website where people throughout the Caucasus region could access the Bible in their own language. As he researched this plan, what he discovered was truly disheartening. Many of the dialects did not have the Scriptures in their language. The limited number of Bibles which existed in regional minority languages were published by companies who adhered to copyright laws, and Dima was denied permission to upload them.

Copyrighted Scripture translations had been a roadblock to Wycliffe Associates' mission as well. When translation teams come together, they require an accurate Bible version in the "gateway" language that is the most familiar second language to the team members. Often the version needed is copyrighted and permission must be granted in order for it to be used as the base upon which a minority project can begin. Permission is sometimes denied and sometimes the process is so tedious it slows the work to a crawl. WA's response to this dilemma is remarkable and a true example of the Lord's mandate: "Freely you and have received; freely give." A dedicated team of Bible scholars and staff have compiled a cache of open-license materials that are made available online for free. Included are Scripture translations in more than forty major gateway languages, as well as other helpful resources.

For the minority dialects young Dima had in mind, Russian was the most common second language to use as a base. A fresh open-license Russian translation was needed, and Dima set his sights on creating one. Since many college-age young people were bilingual in Russian and English, Dima desired to enlist them as co-laborers. He found many who were able and willing, but they were scattered throughout the former Soviet Union. How could they all work together when their work and study schedules made a long-distance meet-up impossible?

Drawing on his years of computer code-writing experience, Dima began to imagine a way to make this possible virtually. He inquired of WA if they would be open to letting him create some software that would allow for distance collaboration. Dima was urged to go ahead and try it. He and another programmer developed an online platform that would guide and assist the translation process. All that was needed for people in the field—any field—to utilize the finished product was an internet connection, a browser, and a secure password. Once a specific translation was completed by a team of collaborators, it could be uploaded to a digital publishing website. All the translations are published under Creative Commons open licensing, enabling anyone who speaks the language to access the translation without cost or limitation.

God allowed Dima to not only see the fulfillment of his heart's desire but to participate in it; making the Scriptures available free of charge to spiritually hungry people in the Caucasus. In fact, this innovation has had a greater impact than Dima ever imagined, expanding to every continent in the world.

Rob's Story, Papua New Guinea

THE CELEBRATION WAS seventeen years in the making. On September 22, 2018, the Doromu-Koki people of Papua New Guinea received the New Testament in their language for the very first time. The Holy Scripture was carried into the church within a decorated "ark" led by a procession of dancing celebrants wearing grass skirts. The long-awaited dedication ceremony featured the reading of selected verses which brought tears to many eyes.

After a showing of the "Jesus Film" (also in the Doromu-Koki language), those in attendance were given the opportunity to purchase their very own precious New Testament bound in red vinyl. An audio version was also available.

Rob Bradshaw knew early in his Christian walk he wanted to be a Bible translator. The idea of providing the living light of God's Word to people living in darkness seemed fulfilling, and intriguing. "I feel that God has called me to this work," he says. "I am so blessed to have God's Word in my language, and He has given me the gifts and ability to help others to have God's Word in their language too." He couldn't imagine spending his life any other way.

Bradshaw prepared for this endeavor by immersing himself in college-level Bible study at his home church, Calvary Chapel in Costa Mesa, California. He spent four years studying linguistics and translation principles at universities in California, Washington, and Texas. In 1987, he was sent out by Wycliffe Bible Translators to Papua New Guinea.

He found life there to be pretty much what he imagined it to be—strange, remote, and rugged. It was also mostly lonely . . . until he met his wife, Betsy, who was also serving on this particular mission field.

Missionary and translator Rob Bradshaw is a living illustration of what we have been looking at in this chapter of *Guardians of the Word*. Having been called and sent by God to serve the people of Papua New Guinea in 1987, Rob has experienced both the "old school" methods of Bible translation and the blessings of utilizing the tools of modern technology. In our correspondence back and forth through email, I asked him some specific questions related to this topic and I have decided to allow him to speak for himself in telling his story.

> SM: How have technological innovations assisted you in your work? I assume it is quite different today than it

was when your work began.

RB: Back when I started in 1987, I had my dictionary on three-by-five cards in a box. Now it is in a computer program in which I can have interaction in every step of the translation process, from language learning and analysis, to drafting, checking, literacy issues, etc. Having electronic commentaries, lexicons and other translation helps has been wonderful. In the early days, all those books had to be carried back and forth. To travel to the Doromu-Koki area I have to hike over very steep mountains and cross rivers, so I can't bring much more than what I can fit in my backpack. The main program I used for translation (Paratext) allowed me to have all those items together in windows that would scroll together. I could look at multiple translations in English, the original languages and other languages too, commentaries, and other helps all at the same time while we were looking at the translation that we were drafting or checking. And now, the Doromu-Koki people can have the New Testament in print form, on Megavoice audio players, online or phone app, and soon their dictionary will be available as well. Printed copies are in the mail right now, the online version is up and running, and the phone app is in production. They can also see the "Jesus Film" in their language online or on SD cards, so they can put it on their phones.

Still, even with the blessed assistance of these tools, some of the challenges to translating the Scriptures for remote people groups still remain the same. In the case of Bradshaw's ministry among the Doromu-Koki people, the inaccessibility of the location still presents logistical problems. Roughly half of these folks reside in the region's capital city of Port Moresby which fortunately is accessible by plane. However, the main village, Kasonomu, is quite isolated—a two-hour bus ride followed by a three-hour rigorous hike in steep terrain. The two-hour estimate for the public transport part of the trip is under the best of conditions. Unexpected variants, such as a flat tire or a bus arriving already overcrowded with no more room for people or necessary equipment, can make the excursion stretch from hours to days. The same holds true for travel on foot; trail conditions or unforeseen physical difficulties of the travelers can greatly hamper progress.

And even with the aid of computers, recording devices, and such, the work itself is still tedious and time-consuming. For example, to create a recorded version of the already translated Doromu-Koki New Testament required forty days and two hundred fifty hours for three native speakers, a recording technician, and Rob as advisor, to complete the task. With the need to re-record parts where the speakers flubbed, there was a bit of tension and urgent prayer as they struggled to finish in the time allotted. In the end, the native speakers decided that Rob's voice needed to be included, so Rob stepped up to read James and Jude for the recording. Having an audio recording of the Scriptures was a paramount blessing for the Doromu-Koki because they are primarily an oral society.

Another on-going struggle is the spiritual opposition which comes when one is doing God's work. Satan, our enemy continues to do what he can to thwart the advance of God's kingdom and discourage God's people. This is true no matter the language, nation, or population in question, but it becomes especially apparent in regions where Satan has established deeply entrenched strongholds of darkness. Rob Bradshaw and his team feel a particular sense of urgency in making the life-changing, liberating Scriptures accessible to the Doromu-Koki. He explains:

> The Doromu-Koki people are animistic, fearing the spirits that inhabit deep pools in the river, mountains,

and other areas deep in the bush. They have been practicing Roman Catholicism since the 1970s yet many still hold onto their magic practices, saying that they can have both. As they continue to read the New Testament and study it, our prayer is that they will see that God has all power over the spirits, and they can have true freedom in Him!

Ramsey's Story, South Sudan

A man's heart plans his way, But the Lord directs his steps. (Proverbs 16:9)

THIS VERSE HAS certainly proved to be true in the life and ministry of Pastor Ramsey Vule. In the 1990s as director of Charis Ministries International based in Nairobi, Kenya, Vule was serving the Lord in his native nation of Sudan. The needs were great, so along with his pastoral ministries of Bible training, evangelistic crusades, and discipleship, he fell into the role of providing logistics for the relief work that was ongoing. Besides distributing food, water wells were drilled, and other community projects were implemented to provide long term improvements in the poverty-stricken nation.

In July 2016, he was in the city of Juba in South Sudan, separated from his family, when yet another civil war struck. Bombs fell. Tanks rolled through. Whole villages were destroyed and set ablaze. The tragic reason for this conflict was political and economic, with a strong undercurrent of generational ethnic animosity. Many were slaughtered. Families were split up as terrorized people fled the violence. It was a tense time for the nation and for the Vule family.

Two hundred thousand refugees ended up in a camp across

the border in northern Kenya. What Ramsey found when he visited the camp was heart-breaking chaos. There were hundreds
of unaccompanied minors wandering the dusty dirt roads. Some
were total orphans—it is amazing that they even made it to the
camp at all. Others had been separated from their family members in the throngs of folks fleeing South Sudan to escape the
violence.

The United Nations (UN) oversaw the massive camp. Meager
food allotments were issued. Housing, consisting of tents or sheet
metal lean-tos, was set up and assigned. But the children—without someone to speak up for their needs—were left homeless
and hungry, minors caring for minors. Ramsey Vule underwent
a ministry shift, becoming an advocate for the many displaced
children. Ramsey and other church elders advised the children
on how to receive UN benefits and even found homes for some
of them with Christian families. He made sure the children under his sponsorship received the food they were entitled to, and
arranged for supplemental food, clothing, and other necessities
to be brought to them through the generosity of Charis Ministry
donors.

As the crisis continued year after year, Pastor Vule grieved
for the children whose entire lives had been turned upside down
with a return to normalcy nowhere on the horizon. He organized
the building of classrooms so that school lessons could at least
resume even though the ratio of teachers to pupils reached 1:400.
Along with that came the obvious need for books. Understand
that throughout Sudan there are over sixty-four tribes representing sixty-four separate language groups. Within each language
there are sub-dialects that could be the heart language of just one
particular village. All those people gathered together in one place
but still unable to successfully communicate with one another.
It was the Tower of Babel all over again. Obtaining or creating

books for the kids to read would be a huge task.

Ramsey decided to start where he could. Fluent in ten languages, he picked a starting point that he felt would captivate the kids and build God's kingdom at the same time. He chose David C. Cook's *Action Bible*. This book, in the style of the modern-day graphic novel, tells the story of the Bible chronologically. He was able to translate the English text of the *Action Bible* into Moru, Ramsey's mother tongue. Field testing his work by reading it to class full of children from this language group, the book was received with enthusiasm. They had never seen anything like this before. One small boy beamed, "This Jesus person speaks in my language!"

Seeing the popularity of this endeavor, seven other men joined Ramsey in the refugee camp to work on other translations for the *Action Bible*. They chose Nuba Moro, one of the languages of the people of the Nuba mountains, to tackle next, dividing the project into manageable portions. Utilizing smart tablets powered by solar panels the team made progress. But there were setbacks. The software they were using to assist with translation did not always "get it right"; they had to revert to "old school" methods for accuracy. And then the paper notebooks containing finished work were attacked! An army of termites came through in the night and ate one-third of the pages.

This did not discourage them. The eight translators resumed work and then the greatest worldwide setback occurred: Corona Virus. Kenya imposed strict lockdowns and curfews on all residents. The UN imposed even tougher restrictions in the refugee camps: no one allowed in or out. These very unusual circumstances did not take God by surprise. Pastor Ramsey Vule has once again found his ministry being redirected by the Lord. For the time being, he is doing virtual ministry and occasionally he is able to coordinate some relief efforts for the widows and orphans in the refugee camps, though he himself is unable to visit them. Translation work, however, continues on the *Action Bible*, though at a snail's pace due to the enforced Covid restrictions.

A Bible version currently exists in both the Moru and Nuba Moro languages (though Ramsey says they are in need of some revisions). But there are other Sudanese tribes who do not yet have the complete Word of God in their own language; among them are the Didinga and the Nyamusa. During this time of lockdown, Vule is offering encouragement to fellow pastors to begin or persevere in translating the Scriptures into the remaining dialects so that everyone can know that this Jesus speaks their language.

Will's Story, Mountainland

> And let us not grow weary while doing good, for in due season we shall reap if we do not lose heart. (Galatians 6:9)

IT'S A GOOD thing that Will and his wife Jennie had this promise to cling to when they first felt the call of God and tried to enter the mission field. In the world's eyes—even the Christian world—they were considered unlikely candidates. When Jennie first turned in her application to become a medical missionary overseas, the agency turned her down as the wrong person for such service.

> And [Will] had an inauspicious start when he achieved a score of fifteen out of a hundred on a language aptitude test; the passing grade was sixty. He could have easily concluded that he was unsuited for such work. Today he is the world's best nonnative speaker of one of the primary [Mountainland] dialects.[130]

Thank God that Will and Jennie, though initially disappointed, did not use this as an excuse to give up. Instead, they persevered. Thank God for His power to overcome obstacles standing in the way of His plan. Thank God that He is able to fully equip those who are willing to be used by Him. The result of God's faithfulness through Will and Jennie is that one of the world's foremost unreached people groups has been exposed to the light of God's great love as revealed by God's own words translated into a language they can understand.

Throughout the history of the Bible there have been regions of the world hostile to the entrance of the light of God's Word. These challenges have a single origin—Satan and his forces of darkness—but various manifestations. Sometimes the opposition and hostilities arise from political or ideological sources, other times by religious strongholds. Such is the case in the world today. These regions can be referred to as "closed" nations as far as the gospel is concerned. Those who attempt to spread the Good News in these locales might become ostracized, unemployed and unable to provide for the basic needs of their families, arrested, imprisoned, beaten, or killed. For these saints, the cost of discipleship is high.

Because the risk is real, privacy must be strictly adhered to when telling the exciting story of Bible translation in the closed region where Will (not his real name) has been serving. Let's call this nation Mountainland.

Those who identify themselves as Mountainlanders number approximately six and a half million and they are located throughout several geographic nations. The literacy rate for these folks is estimated at roughly thirty percent. But the language situation itself among Mountainlanders is complicated. This is because the language is characterized by a multitude of spoken dialects, which contribute to the phenomena that the written language and spoken dialects are *diglossic* or "separate languages."

The prevailing religion in Mountainland is a militant mixture of Buddhism, magic, demon-worship, and tribal sacrifices. Opposition to Christianity comes from religious adherents, government authorities, and a strong sense of nationalism which views any philosophies from the "outside" as a threat. This land has been a coveted prize for missionaries for centuries, but success has been negligible until recently. Will explains:

> Twenty-five years ago, there were no known believers among the 6 million Mountainlanders. In answer to prayer, God began to move among the young people, especially in urban areas. Believers began to write native-language worship songs that were carried across the mountains and played on cassette for seekers. Newly translated Scripture portions were used to reach people, young and old alike. God began to move and now today it can be conservatively estimated that there are 250 + believers in Mountainland itself with a similar number in surrounding nations. New believers continue to write new worship songs and are now reaching other Mountainlanders with the good news of Jesus Christ. Though this recent movement is very encouraging, they are still very much an unreached people group.[131]

This indigenous evangelism has brought with it an urgent plea for God's Word, as you would expect. Will's current work began with the decision to first translate Scripture portions into the written language used by the educated people in the Mountainland culture. This "literary" New Testament translation had its humble beginnings in 1997 with one ex-pat and two nationals. After the initial translation processes from the original languages, checking, rechecking, field testing, and at last preparing for print, the Mountainland New Testament was published in 2015. Five thousand copies have been widely (though secretly) distributed to believers despite the risk involved in doing so. The Scriptures are welcomed as a most cherished possession among those gathering to worship at clandestine house church meetings.

Will's translation team has expanded since the release of the New Testament. Those laboring to complete the finishing touches on the Old Testament now consist of six indigenous and five ex-pat translators working remotely. For accountability, the entire project, including the fund-raising aspect, is being managed by an affiliate of Wycliffe Bible Translators. Donors, translators, technology experts, feet-on-the ground distributors, all working together to bring the life-changing Word of God to people who desperately need to know God loves them.

The complete Mountainland Bible will be available in early 2022, Lord willing. The Bibles will be delivered into the hands of expectant believers and eager evangelists through similar channels as was the Mountainland New Testament; they will need to be hand carried. Due to a tightened security situation in the region in recent years, much prayer is needed for distribution. Should the security situation loosen somewhat, individuals and church groups would be able to form groups and hand carry Bibles into Mountainland.

Thankfully, God's people have once again been able to take advantage of modern technology which can transcend even the most tightly closed borders. An online version of the Mountainland Bible is now available, and soon a version accessible via smart phone apps will be released at no cost to the end user.

But isn't this translation only useful to the thirty percent who are educated, those who can read the literary language? What about the other seventy percent? Will and his team have had these people in their prayers and plans from the start. Simultaneous to the work of translating the Scriptures into the literary language, the team has produced resources in the three major spoken Mountainland dialects. Audio Bibles are already in use in the house churches. Recorded personal testimonies, worship music, and evangelistic tools such as the "Jesus Film" are also in circulation.

> The people who walked in darkness Have seen a great light; Those who dwelt in the land of the shadow of death, Upon them a light has shined. (Isaiah 9:2)

Those labeled "unreached" in a "closed" land are now being touched by the light of God's Word all because an ordinary "unsuitable" man like Will—and others like him—chose to believe what God said.

The Finish Line

AT THE BEGINNING of this chapter, we talked about just how big the job is—a Bible for every language. But it is a job with an end and the end is close at hand. By God's grace, technology has provided some remarkable tools to help reach this goal. God's power, together with willing hearts and hands, will get the blessed task done.

When will the job be done? When will the figure in the column for "number of languages waiting for the Word of God" be zero? Some organizations are boldly predicting the finish line may be as soon as 2025. Certainly, it might be true that the last translator for the last remaining language is alive in the world today. What an exciting time in the history of the Bible!

13

Our Response

Ways to Honor Guardians of the Word

What does all this information mean to you? The reasons for writing *Guardians of the Word* are threefold:

One: It is helpful to understand there is strong evidence the Bible we read today can absolutely be trusted. *Guardians of the Word* establishes (in laymen's terms) that our Bibles are very, very close to the initial, original language words that God breathed to His human scribes. Does your Bible contain the words that lead to everlasting life? Certainly! Does is it hold everything needed to establish godliness and Christlikeness in you? Yes, indeed! (That is, of course, unless your chosen version or paraphrase has been purposely altered to promote a particular human agenda. In which case, please pick a different one for your own spiritual well-being.)

Two: The creation and preservation of God's Word is nothing short of miraculous. And the fact that God used a murderer (Moses), an adulterer (David), a persecutor of the saints (Paul), and one who denied his Lord (Peter), to pen the Scriptures is astonishing. Additionally, God used frail, fallible, weak men such as Wycliffe, Tyndale, Carey, and Townsend to make the Bible available to anyone and everyone. Their stories have been included to show that God calls and equips ordinary people to accomplish remarkable things for His kingdom. He still does this today.

Three: It is my hope and prayer that the information compiled in this book will inspire in you a desire to be faithful to God and to honor His Word. The rest of this chapter will relate some straight forward ways to do this.

The Hall of Faith Bible Heroes

WHY ESTEEM GUARDIANS of the Word? Does admiring people who serve the Lord take away from the praise due to God alone? No, it doesn't seem to. In fact, the Bible itself gives honor to many of the Old Testament saints whose stories are found in its pages.

The great chapter of Hebrews 11 is commonly known as the Hall of Faith. In it, the writer of the Book of Hebrews honors some individuals who accomplished incredible things for God's kingdom. They are commended for their righteousness. Let's take a closer look at some of those mentioned.

Noah— in Hebrews 11:7 Noah is regarded for his obedience to God in building the ark of safety. Noah, his family, and all the animals survived the flood, permitting life on earth to continue. Omitted from this account of Noah's shining moment is the story of how his drunkenness set the stage for an event of shameful incest to occur.

Abraham and Sarah— The Hall of Faith section in verses 8 through 19 tells of Abraham and his beautiful wife Sarah. God called Abraham to leave his comfortable homeland and travel to a distant land, without initially even telling him where the journey would lead. God then promised the aging couple they would be the parents of nations. Though they were both about one hundred years old, they believed this unlikely promise. When at last their long-awaited son Isaac was born, God called upon Abraham to literally sacrifice his son on an altar. Even this Abraham obeyed, and God stayed his hand just before the knife was plunged. For these reasons Abraham is referred to as the Father of Faith.

What it does *not* say is that because of impatience and unbelief Abraham and Sarah conspired together to help God along in the fulfilment of the promise of a son in their old age. Sarah presented her maid Hagar to her husband and that pair had a son, Ishmael. Much trouble ensued from this. Also, there were a couple of episodes where Abraham misrepresented his beautiful wife, saying she was his sister instead of his wife. This put Sarah at risk of abduction and rape in order to save her husband from harm. Today Abraham is recognized as the patriarch of Christianity, Judaism, and Islam. But oh, such a checkered past.

Moses— is commended for eschewing his privileged standing as the adopted son of the pharaoh's daughter. Instead he identified with the oppressed Hebrew slaves of his true ancestry. As their deliverer, Moses instructed the people to appropriate the blood of the Passover lamb as protection against the plague of the slaughter of the firstborn. Then he led them to safety through the miraculous Red Sea crossing. Left out of the Hebrews 11:23-29 account is the time when Moses disobeyed the Lord's direct, specific instructions. Moses was told to speak to a rock in order to provide the nomads on their journey in the wilderness with fresh drinking water. But Moses was irritated by the people's constant complaints and accusations; so instead, he angrily struck the rock twice with his rod. God still provided the water, but Moses' disobedience cost him dearly.

What do Noah, Abraham, Moses, and the others have in common? The Scripture says the things for which they were commended were done in faith. And without faith it is utterly impossible to please God in any way.

> But without faith [it is] impossible to please Him, for he who comes to God must believe that He is, and that He is a rewarder of those who diligently seek Him. (Hebrews 11:6)

Did the good works they performed negate the grievous sins they committed? Definitely not! Their sins were not overlooked because of the "righteous" acts they achieved. On the contrary, God always deals with sin. The shed blood of Jesus on the cross, if it is received by faith, is sufficient to cleanse any sin. However, for those who reject this free gift of salvation and remain unreconciled to God the Father, judgment will ultimately come in that day when they meet Him face to face.

Another thing the Hebrews 11 heroes had in common was their perspective. They filtered everything—their lives, their dreams, their circumstances—through a heavenly lens. They looked at the eternal instead of the temporal. This pleased God. The Bible says:

> These all died in faith, not having received the promises, but having seen them afar off were assured of them, embraced them and confessed that they were strangers and pilgrims on the earth. For those who say such things declare plainly that they seek a homeland . . . But now they desire a better, that is, a heavenly country. Therefore God is not ashamed to be called their God . . . (Hebrews 11:13-14, 16)

How wonderful and gracious our God is in His assessment of these Old Testament saints. This is God's opinion of us as well if we are "in Christ"—that is, if we have put our trust in the saving work of Jesus Christ on the cross. He is not ashamed to be our God, for He no longer sees our sins and failures. Instead He looks at our faith (as weak and feeble as it might be) and sees us as righteous. What a cause for thankful rejoicing!

Honoring Guardians of the Word

So, WITH THE precedent established in the Scriptures, it is right and proper that we esteem those believers throughout history who have faithfully preserved, translated, and disseminated the Holy Word of God to a waiting world. Their stories have honored God and inspired us.

What is the next step?

Educate yourself. Read more about the faithful saints mentioned in this book and others like them. There are many excellent Christian biographies available. A good beginning for easy-to-read publications is Dave and Neta Jackson's *The Complete Book of Christian Heroes*, or their Trailblazer series of individual missionary biographies suitable for all ages. [http://www.trailblazerbooks.com/Frame-1.html] YWAM's missionary story series *Christian Heroes Then and Now* is also excellent. [https://www.christianbook.com/page/homeschool/hs-books/christian-heroes-then-and-now] In addition there are several public domain collections available for Amazon's Kindle which are free of charge.

Educate others. You can easily pass these books along to friends and family members. Even those who are reluctant to read the Bible might be open to a well-written true adventure story. Most definitely share them with your children. Who knows what aspirations might be kindled. You might be like Mrs. Moffat planting seeds in the heart of young Robert. (See chapter 9)

There are also some edifying films on the lives of Christian heroes throughout history. Some that have been meaningful to me are *The Hiding Place*—Corrie ten Boom's time in a Nazi concentration camp; *The End of the Spear*— hat happened after the five missionaries were slaughtered by the Aucas; and *Amazing Grace*—the conversion of William Wilberforce and his subsequent fight to abolish slavery in Britain. Often these videos are available at your local library. What a fun way to spend a meaningful evening with friends.

There are still guardians of the Word in our midst. Yes, there are still Bible translators and support personnel at work today. They work in jungle huts as well as fully equipped offices; far away or maybe next door; both old and young; and from every nation imaginable. These are the folks we have focused on in this book.

However, also to be considered are the missionaries, evangelists, Sunday school teachers, and faithful pastors—these, too, are guardians of the great and holy Word of God. I'm sure if you think for a few minutes some specific individuals will come to mind. God probably has some suggestions for you. These have put their hands to the plow and have not turned back no matter the hardship, struggle, or personal sacrifice. They are worthy of our honor and respect as well.

These workers might often labor with the unwanted companions of loneliness, discouragement, or opposition. But you can help lighten their load or "lift their hands" as Aaron and Hur did for Moses when he was weary (Exodus 17:8-13). There are simple but effective ways to do this. First and foremost—pray for them regularly. "The effective fervent prayer of a righteous man [or woman] avails much" (James 5:16). Ask them how you might pray for them. If they have a newsletter, ask to be put on their mailing or email list.

Secondly, speak or write personal words of encouragement to them. Whether you communicate face to face, by phone, text, email, or social media, they will know you care, and that God cares for them through you. Trust me, this will bless them greatly.

Finally, help these serving saints or their ministries financially if you are able. Give once or give regularly. Give a little or a lot. Give in obedience to the prompting of the Lord. This act will certainly help their work, but it will also help you connect with them as a true partner, sharing in the work. And yes, this is how a missionary or a pastor on the receiving end of your gift truly views you.

Honoring the Word

THE GREATEST/MOST IMPORTANT way to honor guardians of the Word is to honor the Word of God itself. Respecting the Bible is something that must be done personally, individually, from the heart. Provided here are some steppingstones for you to follow as you start down the path of honoring God's Word. These suggestions are to be done with the power and strength God provides through His Holy Spirit. And if there should happen to be detours or occasions of stumbling along the way, remember God's grace is readily at hand for the believer.

Read it! There are various ways to read the Bible. Read it straight through to get a basic understanding of God and His ways. Read to discover truths about a particular topic you want to know more about. An example of this is to take a concordance or Bible index and look up a particular word such as *faith*. This is a quick way to see what the Bible has to say on a specific subject. A systematic Bible reading method called inductive study is a most beneficial Bible reading method. Select a book in the Bible and read it from the beginning. This will give you the context of what is being said. Take for example the Book of Philippians. Right away you will learn it is a letter written by Paul to people he knew in Philippi. In reading the Philippian believers' mail you can discover what issues they were having and the ways Paul, under the inspiration of the Spirit, instructed them to respond. He also offered them encouragement and some exhortations. These truths can then be applied to your own life as God directs. You can learn more about this effective method at https://www.logos.com/how-to/inductive-bible-study.

The most important aspect in reading the Bible is to make it a regular habit. Whether you choose to read the Scriptures in the morning, in the evening, or maybe on your lunch break, consistency is the key. It has been said anything that you do eight days in a row is on its way to becoming a habit. This holds true for the best of routines. Whether you call it devotions, quiet time, or by some other name, make it your practice to read the Bible daily.

Trust it! Believe what it says is true. *Guardians of the Word* has provided a foundation for the trustworthiness of the Scriptures. The Bible contains everything any person needs for life and godliness. Most essential of all is to believe what it says about the need to be born again so you can be saved. Here is a summary of direct passages on this vital topic from the Book of Romans:

> Romans 3:23—For all have sinned and fall short of the glory of God . . .

> Romans 6:23—For the wages of sin is death, but the gift of God *is* eternal life in Christ Jesus our Lord.

> Romans 10:9-10—That if you confess with your mouth the Lord Jesus and believe in your heart that God has raised Him from the dead, you will be saved. For with the heart one believes unto righteousness, and with the

mouth confession is made unto salvation.

Romans 5:1—Therefore, having been justified by faith, we have peace with God through our Lord Jesus Christ . . .

If you have never confessed your sins to God and asked Him to forgive and cleanse you through the sacrifice of His Son Jesus, I urge you to seriously consider the truths in these verses right now—today. Your eternity is at stake. Get alone with God and do business with your Maker. He is waiting to be reconciled to His wayward son or daughter.

Be transformed! As you read the Bible, allow it to do its work of conviction and exhortation. God desires each of His children to reflect the character of His only begotten Son Jesus.

> But we all, with unveiled face, beholding as in a mirror the glory of the Lord, are being transformed into the same image from glory to glory, just as by the Spirit of the Lord. (2 Corinthians 3:18)

This change in us is a work of the Holy Spirit which takes place from the inside out resulting in a total change of heart. The best way for us to behold the Lord in His glory is in the pages of the Holy Bible. This transformation is accomplished when the things we put into our minds (God's words) begin to alter our thought processes, then our attitudes, and lastly our actions.

> And do not be conformed to this world, but be transformed by the renewing of your mind, that you may prove what is that good and acceptable and perfect will of God. (Romans 12:2)

As you come to understand what God is like and the way He desires for you to live your life, it is logical that the very next step in your Bible journey is to . . .

Obey it! "Do the dos and don't do the don'ts." Do what it says! Read it, yes. Learn about God in the Bible – yes. But if that is as far as it goes, you will be a miserable and ineffective Christian. Instead—

> But be doers of the word, and not hearers only, deceiving yourselves. For if anyone is a hearer of the word and not a doer, he is like a man observing his natural face in a mirror; for he observes himself, goes away, and immediately forgets what kind of man he was. But he who looks into the perfect law of liberty and continues [in it], and is not a forgetful hearer but a doer of the work, this one will be blessed in what he does. (James 1:22-25)

The Holy Spirit is readily available to help you stay on the path. You can pray along with the psalmist:

> Direct my steps by Your word, And let no iniquity have dominion over me. (Psalm 119: 133)

Share it! The Bible is a wonderful, beautiful, remarkable, life-giving, life-changing book. It provides light in a dark, dark world. In its pages we learn about our magnificent Heavenly Father. We learn about the Way He has provided for us to be reconciled to Him through His Son Jesus. It tells us what heaven is like and how we can live there forever with Him. Along the way we receive strength, comfort, and help in times of trouble. Don't keep this Good News to yourself!

When you get together with believing Christian friends, make God's Word part of the conversation. Share with someone what God has been showing you in His Word lately. Ask them what they have been learning. This is true fellowship.

God might bring a Scripture verse to your mind that could be just the thing to help a struggling brother or sister stay on the path. Share it!

Be ready and available to share the truth of God's Good News message with those who don't yet know Jesus. A verse or two of comfort or instruction may well be the prompt that a searching soul needs to take another step toward the truth. Share it! You have this promise from the Lord that your efforts will not be wasted—

For as the rain comes down,
and the snow from heaven,
And do not return there, But water the earth,
And make it bring forth and bud,
That it may give seed to the sower
And bread to the eater,
So shall My word be that goes forth from My mouth;
It shall not return to Me void,
But it shall accomplish what I please,
And it shall prosper [in the thing] for which I sent it.
(Isaiah 55:10-11)

---

*All Scripture is given by inspiration
of God, and is profitable
for doctrine, for reproof,
for correction, for instruction in
righteousness, that the man of
God may be complete, thoroughly
equipped for every good work.*
2 Timothy 3:16-17

Appendix

The Apocrypha: a collection of disputed books

A COMPARISON OF a Catholic Bible with a typical Protestant Bible is bound to cause some confusion or curiosity. What are those extra books in there? Known either as the Apocrypha (which means hidden) or deutro-canonical (second canon) these books were chiefly written in the era between the completion of the Old Testament and the beginning of the New. The books included in this collection fluctuated throughout various years and according to different geographic traditions. A sampling of contents is listed here:

Wisdom of Solomon	1 Maccabees	Susanna
Sirach	2 Maccabees	Bel and the Dragon
Tobit	Baruch	Prayer of Manasseh
Judith	Letter of Jeremiah	Additions to Daniel
Prayer of Azariah	Additions to Esther	

The Jews were aware of this collection of literature, but never esteemed the works as canonical. The early Christian church, likewise, regarded the Apocrypha as interesting reading and useful for some historical background, but none of the writings were used for the edification of the church the way Scripture was. Confusion began to set in around the time of the Reformation as some of the Protestant Bibles inserted the Apocrypha as a supplement though not as part of the Bible itself—including Martin Luther's German translation, and the earliest editions of the King James Bible.

In 1546 at the Council of Trent, the Roman Catholic Church officially declared eleven of the deutro-canonical books to be sacred text. They issued this statement: "If anyone should not accept the said books as sacred . . . let him be anathema [forever cursed.]"[132] The Second Ecumenical Council of the Vatican (Vatican 2) convened in 1962-1965 upheld and reconfirmed this proclamation.

When all is said and done, to elevate any or all the disputed books of the Apocrypha to the same position as God-breathed Scripture is to skew the test of canonicity in such a way that the church itself is given greater authority than the Bible. Does the church determine and regulate what is Scripture or does the church discover and recognize what is Scripture? Is the church master over the Bible or is the Bible master over the church?

Clearly, these two philosophies are completely contradictory, and a Bible-reader will need Holy Spirit guided discernment to determine which is the right viewpoint. In addition, the writings of the Apocrypha fail the tests of canonicity discussed in chapter 1—authorship, inspiration, and acceptance.

Endnotes

Chapter 1: In the Beginning . . . It is Finished

1. https://www.deadseascrolls.org.il/learn-about-the-scrolls/discovery-and-publication?locale=en_US, accessed April 8, 2021.

2. http://www.deadseascrolls.org.il/learn-about-the-scrolls/scrolls-content, accessed April 8, 2021.

3. David Hocking, *The History and Authenticity of the Bible*, taken from the transcript, page 93, https://www.blbi.org/library/pdf/031_00.pdf

4. W. Kenneth Connolly, *The Indestructible Book: The Bible, Its Translators, and Their Sacrifices*, Baker Books, Grand Rapids, Michigan, 1996, page 15, 16.

5. W. H. Griffith Thomas, *How We Got Our Bible*, Moody Press, 1926, page 13-14.

6. W. Kenneth Connolly, page 13.

7. Ibid., page 16.

8. Ibid., page 17.

9. Ibid.

10. W. H. Griffith Thomas, page 14-15.

11. W. Kenneth Connolly, page 30.

12. Wayne Gruden, *Systematic Theology*, Zondervan Publishing, Grand Rapids, MI, 1994, page 6.

13. F. F. Bruce, *The New Testament Documents: Are They Reliable?*, Grand Rapids, Eerdmans, 1960, page 27.

14. David Hocking, T*he History and Authenticity of the Bible,* taken from the transcript, page 265, https://www.blbi.org/library/pdf/031_00.pdf.

15. W. H. Griffith Thomas, page 25.

16. Dr. Norman Geisler, *Systematic Theology, Volume 1*, Introduction, Bible, Bethany House Publishers, Bloomington, MN, 2002, page 539.

17. W. Kenneth Connolly, page 48.

Chapter 2: John Wycliffe

18. Harry Emerson Fosdick, *Great Voices of the Reformation*, Ransom

House, New York, 1952, page 5.

19. W. Kenneth Connolly, *The Indestructible Book: The Bible, Its Translators, and Their Sacrifices,* Baker Books, Grand Rapids, Michigan, 1996, page 73.

20. Ibid., page 74.

21. Brian Moynahan, *God's Bestseller,* St. Martin's Press, New York, 2002, page xiii.

22. Ibid., page xvii.

23. Ibid., page xviii.

24. Harry Emerson Fosdick, page 10.

25. W. Kenneth Connolly, page 79.

26. Ibid., page 78.

27. John Foxe, *Foxe's Book of Martyrs,* Lighthouse Trails Publishing, Eureka, MT, 2010, page 157.

28. Harry Emerson Fosdick, page 8.

Chapter 3: The Reformers

29. W. Kenneth Connolly, *The Indestructible Book: The Bible, Its Translators, and Their Sacrifices,* Baker Books, Grand Rapids, Michigan, 1996, page 91.

30. Ibid., page 90.

31. https://www.britannica.com/biography/Desiderius-Erasmus

32. Lyndal Roper, *Martin Luther: Renegade and Prophet,* Random House, New York, 2016, page xx.

33. Ibid., page xxvii.

34. John Foxe, *Foxe's Book of Martyrs,* Lighthouse Trails Publishing, Eureka, MT, 2010, page 171.

35. Ibid., page 172.

36. http://www.luther.de/en/worms.html

37. *Library of the World's Best Literature,* edited by Charles Dudley Warner, Vol. XXIII, J. A. Hill and Co., 1896, page 9332.

38. Lyndal Roper, page 196.

39. http://www.thenagain.info/WebChron/WestCiv/Erasmus.html

accessed April 8, 2021.

40. Roger Oakland, The Good Shepherd Calls, Lighthouse Trails Publishing, Eureka, MT, 2017, page 56.

41. William Hazlitt, translator; The Table Talk or Familiar Discourse of Martin Luther, London, David Bogue, 1848, page 1.

Chapter 4: William Tyndale

42. Brian Moynahan, God's Bestseller: William Tyndale, Thomas More, and the Writing of the English Bible—A Story of Martyrdom and Betrayal, St. Martin's Press, New York, 2002, page 18.

43. Brian H. Edwards, God's Outlaw: The Story of William Tyndale and the English Bible, Evangelical Press, Hertfordshire, England, 1976, page 49.

44. Ibid., page 31.

45. Ibid., page 62.

46. Ibid., page 71.

47. Ibid., page 82.

48. Ibid., page 97.

49. Ibid., page 90.

50. Ibid.

51. Ibid., page 91.

52. Ibid., page 100.

53. Brian Moynahan, page 73.

54. Ibid., page 104.

55. Ibid., page 233.

56. Ibid., page 179.

57. Ibid.

58. Harry Freeman, The Murderous History of Bible Translations: Power, Conflict and the Quest for Meaning, Bloomsbury Press, New York, 2016, page 109.

59. Brian H. Edwards, page 100.

60. Ibid., page 168.

61. Ibid., page 145.

Chapter 5: The King James Version

62. Brian H. Edwards, *God's Outlaw: The Story of William Tyndale and the English Bible*, Evangelical Press, Hertfordshire, England, 1976, page 170.

63. W. Kenneth Connolly, *The Indestructible Book: The Bible, Its Translators, and Their Sacrifices*, Baker Books, Grand Rapids, Michigan, 1996, page 148.

64. Ibid., page 152.

65. John Foxe, *Foxe's Book of Martyrs*, Lighthouse Trails Publishing, Eureka, MT, 2010, page 219.

66. Alister McGrath, *In the Beginning: The Story of the King James Bible and How it Changed a Nation, a Language, and a Culture*, Anchor Books, New York, 2001, page 135.

67. Ibid., page 138.

68. Ibid., page 140.

69. Ibid., page 160-161.

70. Ibid., page 163-164.

71. Ibid., page 173-175.

72. Ibid., page 177.

73. Ibid., page 194.

Chapter 6: The Art of Translation

74. David Hocking, *The History and Authenticity of the Bible*, taken from the transcript, page 134, https://www.blbi.org/library/pdf/031_00.pdf.

75. Edward D. Andrews, *The Complete Guide to Bible Translation: Bible Translation Choices and Translation Principles*, Christian Publishing House, Cambridge, Oh, 2016, page 129-135.

76. David Hocking, page 312.

77. Preface to New King James Bible, Thomas Nelson, 1992, page v-vi.

78. Scott J. Duvall and Daniel J. Hays, *Grasping God's Word: A Hands-On Approach to Reading, Interpreting, and Applying the Bible*, Zondervan, Kindle location 494.

79. Edward D. Andrews, Tpage 150.

80. https://www.breadcrumbsministries.org/text-types--bible-translations.html

81. Jack Popjes, *The Why and How of Bible Translation: What Every Christian Should Know*, Expanded Edition, 2018, page 39.

82. Jack Popjes, *The Why and How of Bible Translation: What Every Christian Should Know*, Expanded Edition, 2018.

83. Ibid., page 75-76.

Chapter 7: Go Ye Therefore

84. Jack Popjes, *The Why and How of Bible Translation: What Every Christian Should Know*, Expanded Edition, 2018, page 27.

85. Ibid.

86. Matt K. Matsuda, *Pacific Worlds: a history of seas, peoples and cultures*, 2012, Cambridge University Press, page 136.

87. Ibid., page **145**.

88. Eugene Myers Harrison, *Giants of the Missionary Trail.* Originally published by Scripture Press, Book Division, 1954, https://www.wholesomewords.org/missions/giants/bionott.html

89. https://en.wikipedia.org/wiki/Samuel_Marsden

90. https://www.wholesomewords.org/missions/giants/biomarsden.html

91. https://biblesociety.org.nz/discover-the-bible/the-bible-in-maori/

92. https://biblesociety.org.nz/wp-content/uploads/2018/10/The-Bibles-early-journey-in-New-Zealand.pdf, page 6.

93. Ibid., page 7.

94. *The Life and Diary of David Brainerd*, edited by Jonathan Edwards, Moody Bible Institute, Chicago, 1949 (with a biographical sketch of the life and work of Jonathan Edwards by Philip E. Howard Jr.), Baker Book House, Grand Rapids, MI, 1989, page 119.

95. https://gfamissions.org/pages/learn-and-promote/detail/3/21/

96. *The Life and Diary of David Brainerd*, page 186.

97.https://www.thegospelcoalition.org/article/diary-of-a-life-on-the-brink-of-eternity/

Chapter 8: William Carey

98. https://www.wholesomewords.org/missions/giants/biocarey2.html

99. Timothy George, *Faithful Witness: the Life and Mission of William*

Carey, Christian History Institute, 1998, page 32-33.

100. George Smith, *Life of William Carey,* R & R Clark, Edinburgh, 1909, digital location 40758 of 25 Classic Christian Biographies.

101. Timothy George, page 82.

102. Ibid., page 78.

103. Ibid., page 87.

104. Ibid., page 131.

105. Ibid., page 139

106. Ibid., page 140.

107. Ibid., page 173.

108. Ibid., back cover.

109. Ibid.

Chapter 9: To All the World

110. https://www.christianpost.com/news/adoniram-judson-endurance-personified-in-the-life-of-burmas-first-protestant-missionary-from-north-america.html

111. Florence Huntington Jensen, *Hearts Aflame*, Waukesha, Wisc.: Metropolitan Church Assn., ©1932.

112. Thomas John Bach, *Pioneer Missionaries for Christ and His Church,* Van Kampen Press, Wheaten, IL, 1955.

113. Thomas John Bach, *Pioneer Missionaries for Christ and His Church,* Van Kampen Press, Wheaten, IL, 1955.

114. Walls, "A Second Narrative of Samuel Ajayi Crowther's Early Life," Bulletin of the Society for African History 2 (1965): 14.

115.https://www.history.ox.ac.uk/samuel-ajayi-crowther-black-victorians-and-the-future-of-africa

Chapter 10: Hudson Taylor

116. https://www.wholesomewords.org/missions/biotaylor15.html

117. https://www.goodreads.com/quotes/741391-the-weaver-my-life-is-but-a-weaving-between-my

Chapter 11: Cameron Townsend & Wycliffe Bible Translators

118. James & Marti Hefley, *Uncle Cam,* Mott Media, Milford, MI, 1981, page 31.

119. Ibid., page 33.

120. Ibid., page. 43.

121. Ibid., page 48.

122. Ibid., page 74.

123. Ibid., page 118-9.

124. Ibid., page 122.

125. https://www.colineharnson.com/dayuma/

126. Ibid.

Chapter 12: The Impact of Technology & Contemporary Guardians

127. https://thebibleanswer.org/how-many-languages-bible-translated-into/

128. Wycliffe Associates (WA) was founded in 1967 as a subgroup within Wycliffe Bible Translators (WBT) (now Wycliffe USA). In 2016 WA split off from WBT and became an entirely separate entity. The detachment occurred when distinct differences in translation protocols and philosophies became irreconcilable.

129. https://thedigitalbiblelibrary.org/

130. Thomas Hale, *A Light Shines in Central Asia*, William Carey Library, Pasadena, CA, 2002, page 161.

131. Personal correspondence, edited for security reasons.

Appendix: The Apocrypha

132. Dr. Norman Geisler, *Systematic Theology, Volume 1*, Introduction, Bible, Bethany House Publishers, Bloomington, MN, 2002, page 515.

About the Author

SUSAN MOORE HAS had articles published in magazines and newspapers, and served as a writing assistant and ghostwriter. An editor for more than thirty years, her projects include more than a dozen full-length manuscripts and countless articles. She owns and operates Page & Pixel Publications which offers editing services as well as book design for print or digital publication. Susan is a world traveler who currently lives in Wisconsin with her husband of forty-eight years.

Books & Booklets by Susan Moore

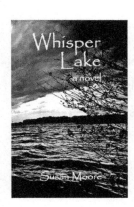

WHISPER LAKE: A NOVEL

A RIVETING TALE OF SPIRITUAL WARFARE. Whisper Lake appears to be a typical community with its share of peace and troubles. But behind the scenes the demon realm is making dangerous inroads into the very fabric of the community. When a miracle occurs, the entire town is captivated and searching for answers. This leaves the clergymen of Whisper Lake polarized. Is this a sign from God or the work of something sinister? Available on Amazon.

BOOKLET TRACTS

7 REASONS THE BIBLE CAN BE TRUSTED

REMEMBERING THE PERSECUTED CHURCH

Kindle editions available on Amazon.

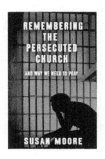

Need help with your manuscript?
Professional Services Offered

- Editing
- Writing/Rewriting
- Book Design
- eBook Formatting
- Proofreading
- Manuscript Evaluation
- Consultation

Contact:
Page & Pixel Publications
www.pageandpixelpublications.com
pageandpixelpublications@gmail.com